Crafts

Under Construction

Standard PUBLISHING

CINCINNATI, OHIO

CONTENTS

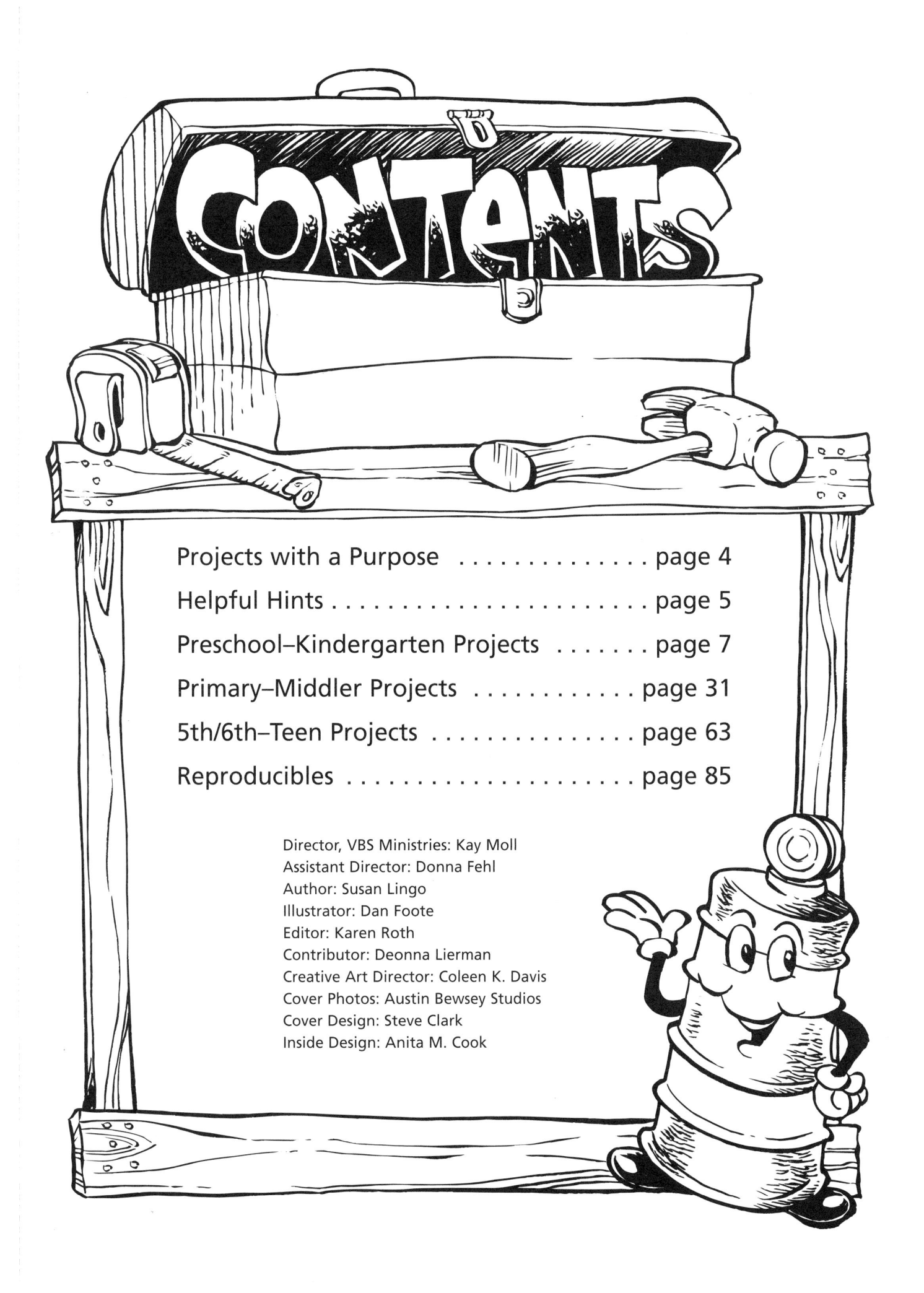

Projects with a Purpose . . . . page 4

Helpful Hints . . . . page 5

Preschool–Kindergarten Projects . . . . page 7

Primary–Middler Projects . . . . page 31

5th/6th–Teen Projects . . . . page 63

Reproducibles . . . . page 85

Director, VBS Ministries: Kay Moll
Assistant Director: Donna Fehl
Author: Susan Lingo
Illustrator: Dan Foote
Editor: Karen Roth
Contributor: Deonna Lierman
Creative Art Director: Coleen K. Davis
Cover Photos: Austin Bewsey Studios
Cover Design: Steve Clark
Inside Design: Anita M. Cook

PROJECTS WITH A PURPOSE

Kids love crafts! They're fun, exciting, and a wonderful outlet for young, creative minds. But crafts can be so much more. These projects can serve as important tools to building character, knowledge, and ability. Remind yourself of the benefits of crafts before you gather your supplies.

Crafts teach:
- responsibility for materials, tools, and cleanup.
- discipline of completing a project.
- independence of work skills.
- teamwork in sharing materials, tools, and space.

Crafts develop:
- creativity—there is no "right" way.
- confidence—"I did it myself."
- enjoyment of simple, inexpensive activities.
- basic physical skills, using different muscle groups.

Crafts bring to mind:
- church as a happy place.
- teachers as special people.
- a favorite Scripture verse or Bible story.
- ideas to worship God.
- the plan of salvation.

HELPFUL HINTS

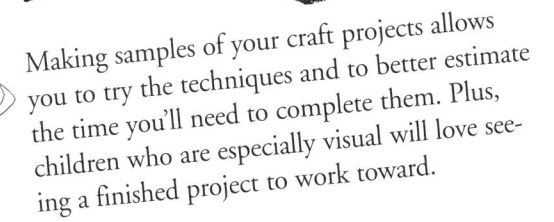

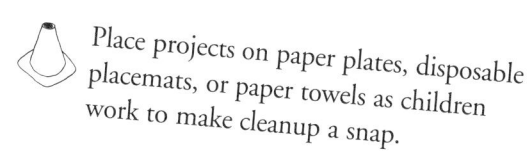

Making samples of your craft projects allows you to try the techniques and to better estimate the time you'll need to complete them. Plus, children who are especially visual will love seeing a finished project to work toward.

Place projects on paper plates, disposable placemats, or paper towels as children work to make cleanup a snap.

Help children carry their projects home safely. Large grocery or lunch sacks, boxes, or even plastic bags keep craft items dry and avoid breakage.

Kids love making and using their own personal craft aprons! For each apron, simply staple a dozen paper towels in a stack. Then stick a 3-foot length of masking tape at the top edge of each stack. Fold the tape over and tie as apron "strings." As each paper towel is used, simply tear it off to make a fresh apron.

Stick self-adhesive hook-and-loop fasteners on plastic serving trays. Stick the corresponding fastener pieces to glue bottles, marker cans, scissors, or other craft supplies. When kids carry the trays to the tables, nothing will fall off or become lost!

Keep cans of hairspray handy to add a protective coating over crayon, chalk, or charcoal drawings and projects. It cuts down the "smudge factor" and adds a light protective coating without the stickiness of spray shellac.

Wash out roll-on deodorant bottles and fill them with nail polish remover. (Just pop out the roller balls and replace them after filling.) Children love cleaning markers, glue, and crayons off tables with these bottles. Just be sure children wash their hands afterward.

Preschool Kindergarten

Preschoolers
- Can't sit still for very long.
- Learn by doing and by repetition.
- Learn by touching, tasting, smelling, seeing, and hearing.
- Are learning to share, help, and take turns.
- Have not mastered scissors, coloring in lines, or folding on lines.

Kindergartners
- Enjoy a variety of methods and materials.
- Can use scissors, glue, large crayons, and large paintbrushes.
- Love to laugh and giggle and may be mischievous.
- Like to ask, "Why?" and want to have reasons for what they are doing.
- Seek approval from adults for their behavior and their craft projects.

So . . .
- Remember that the process is more important than the finished product.
- Choose appropriate projects that the student (not the teacher) can finish.
- Be especially aware of choking hazards, as some little people like to put things in their mouths.
- Be prepared with coverings and clean-up materials. Some messiness is inevitable.
- Share the love of Jesus in your attitude, voice, and actions.

Darrel the Barrel Sit-Upon

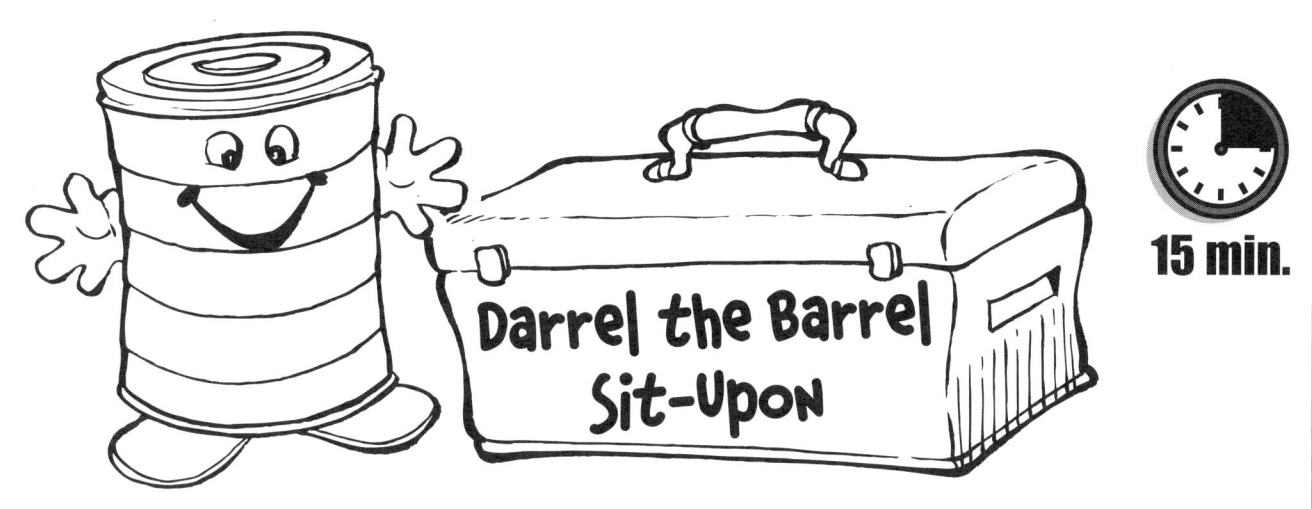

15 min.

Pre-K

Grab Your Gear:
- large popcorn tins (1 per child)
- orange, white, pink, yellow, black, and blue felt or craft foam
- colored craft foam shapes (circles and triangles)
- scissors
- tacky craft glue (or hot glue gun for adult use only)
- black permanent markers
- Darrel the Barrel patterns from page 10
- photocopier

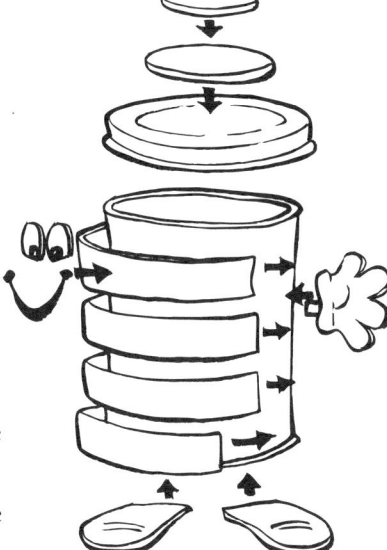

Before class, cut three orange felt or craft foam strips to fit around each tin. Cut two white felt or foam strips to go around each tin. Cut one circle of orange felt or foam to fit the top center area of each lid. Cut one 4" circle of yellow felt or foam as the "light" for each lid. Use the patterns from page 10 to precut Darrel's facial features, hands, and feet from felt or foam. Cut two 1½" x 2½" strips of black foam for each child to use as Darrel's arms.

Get to Work:

1. Distribute the popcorn tins. Open and close each tin several times to loosen the seal. (This makes it easier to work with the tin.)
2. Using tacky glue, attach the orange circle to the center of the lid. Then glue the yellow circle in the center of the orange circle. Set aside to dry.
3. Glue the orange and white felt or foam strips around the tin. Position the bottom strip so that it sits on the bottom rim. Leave about an inch at the top of the tin to allow for the lid. The top and bottom strips should be orange, alternating with white in between. (See cover photo.)
4. After the tin is covered, make Darrel's face using felt or craft foam shapes. (See cover photo.) Then attach his arms, hands, and feet. Replace the lid when dry.

Hammer It Home

Using the Darrel the Barrel Sit-Upons, play a quick game of Simon Says. Use instructions such as, "Simon says tap your Sit-Upon two times" or "Simon says hop around your Sit-Upon." End by having Simon tell kids to sit on their Sit-Upons; then tell kids that when they do as they're told, they're obeying. Remind them that God wants them to always obey Him and do as the Bible says. Explain that obeying God's Word will help them build strong, happy lives for Him!

BLUE

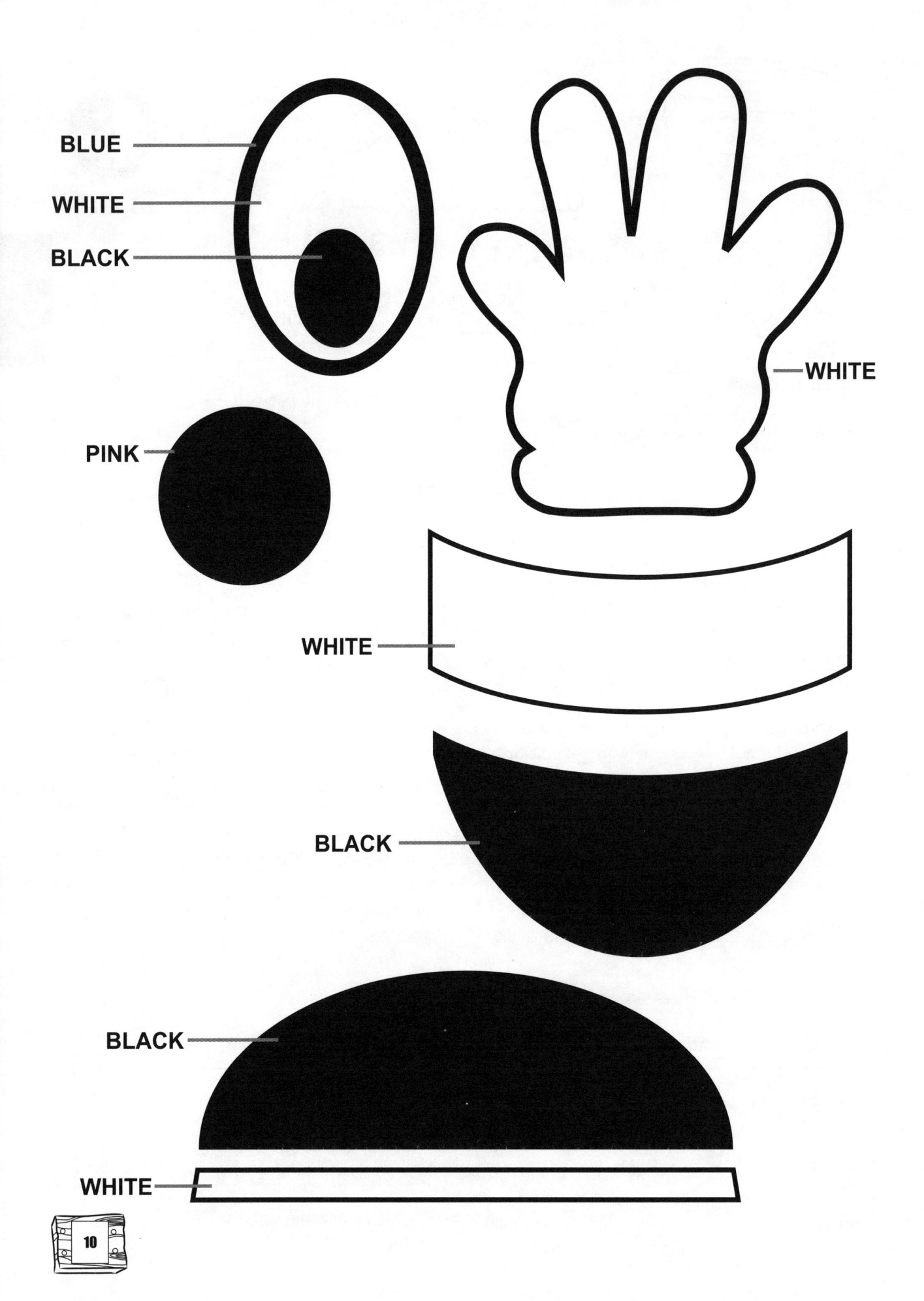

WHITE

BLACK

WHITE

PINK

WHITE

BLACK

BLACK

WHITE

20 min.

Grab Your Gear:
- bright yellow plastic salad or mixing bowls (1 per child)
- small, red bicycle reflectors (1 per child)
- hot glue gun with glue (for adult use only)
- permanent markers
- bright yellow craft foam
- scissors
- stickers or self-adhesive craft foam shapes (optional)
- self-adhesive hook-and-loop fasteners
- hat bill and chin strap patterns from page 12

Get to Work:
1. Cut the bills and chin straps from yellow craft foam, adjusting the size as needed to fit your plastic bowls. Attach a bill to each bowl using a hot glue gun.
2. Glue a bicycle reflector to the front of the hat using a hot glue gun. (Children can hold them in place as they dry.)
3. Write each child's name on the hat under the reflector using permanent markers or self-adhesive letters.
4. Add decorations and designs to the hat using the markers. Use stickers or self-adhesive craft foam shapes to embellish the hat if desired.
5. Glue one end of the yellow chin strap to one inside edge of the bowl. On the opposite side, attach one portion of a self-adhesive hook-and-loop fastener. Attach the matching fastener piece to the other end of the strap so that it will hook in place when worn.

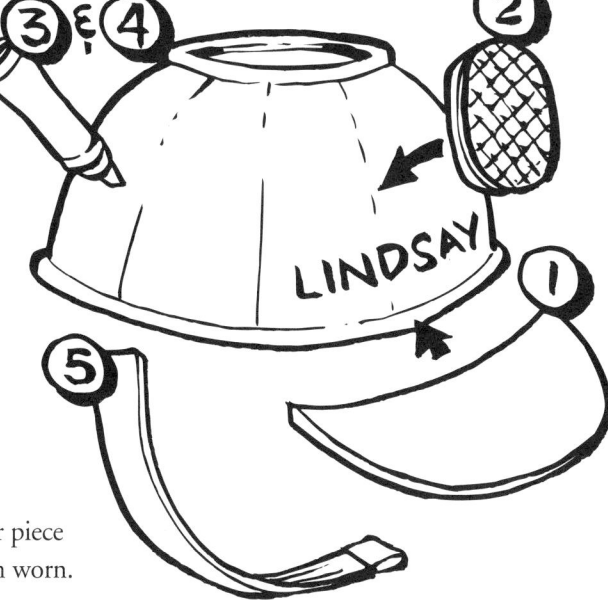

Hammer It Home

Have children put on their hard hats. Then ask them what hard hats do. Explain that hard hats protect people from being hurt while they're building things. Then tell children that Jesus protects them too, as they're building their lives for Him. Have children march around the room while wearing their Hard Hats and singing "Jesus Loves Me." If there's time, substitute the words *saves* and *protects* in place of the word *loves*.

12

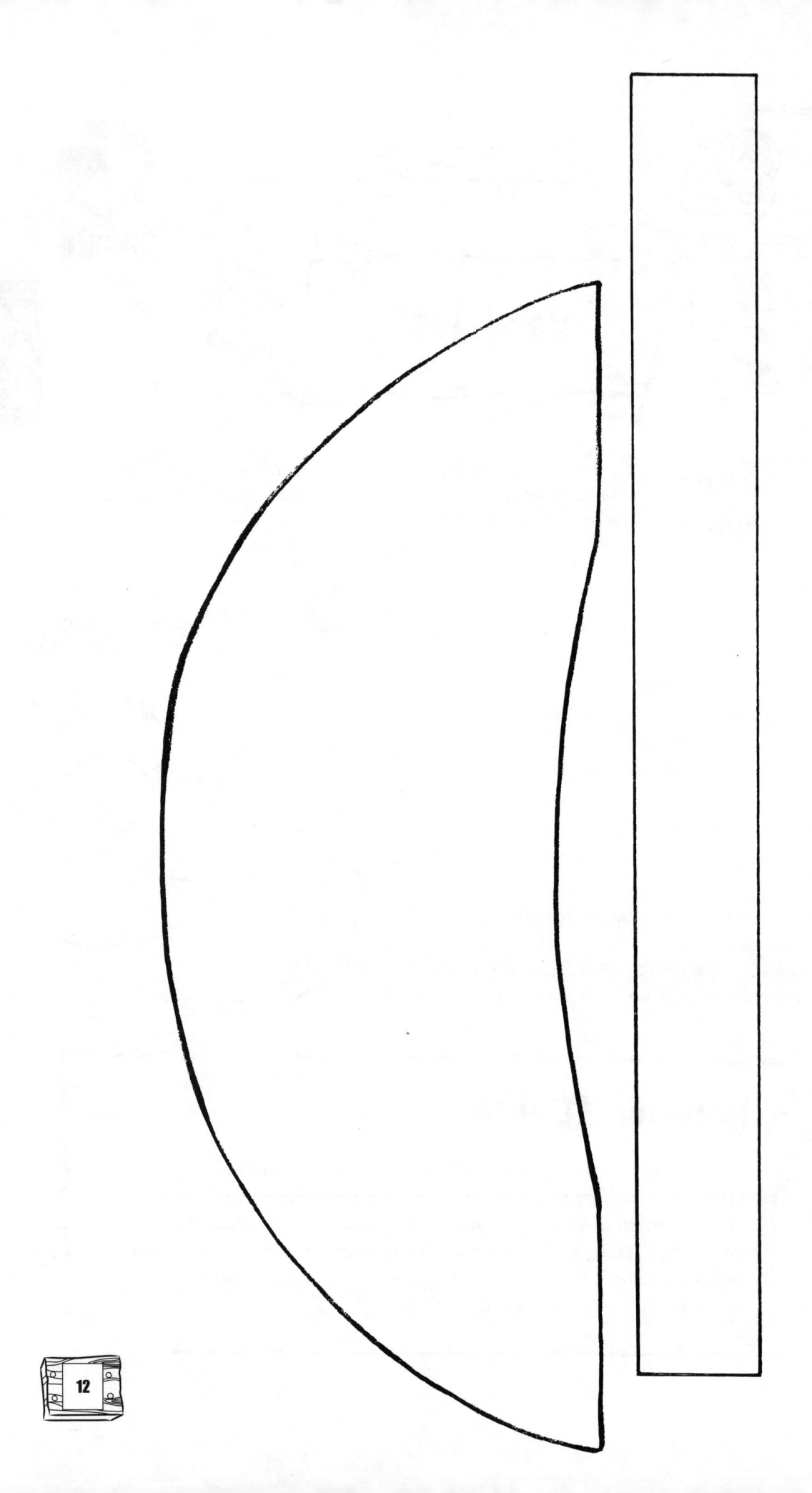

Away in a Manger Suncatchers

20 min.

Pre-K

Grab Your Gear:
- clear plastic dinner plates (2 per child)
- tempera paints (blue, yellow, and red)
- tacky craft glue
- scissors
- craft sticks (4 per child)
- washable markers
- tape
- fishing line
- star and manger patterns from page 14
- stiff white paper
- photocopier

Get to Work:

1. Photocopy the patterns onto stiff white paper (one set per child). Cut out the mangers and stars.

2. Give each child two clear plastic plates. Show children how to drop several small pools of tempera paint onto the concave side of one of their plates. Then add about ½ teaspoon craft glue to the paints and swirl the mixture around with craft sticks.

3. Nest the other plates on top of the paint and glue swirls. (One plate should actually be stacked inside the other with the swirls caught between the two plates.) Set the plates aside to dry for a few minutes.

4. Color the craft sticks using brown markers. Then glue the sticks together, forming a triangle.

5. Distribute paper mangers and stars; color them with markers. Glue stars to one point of the triangles, and then glue the mangers to the craft sticks opposite the stars.

6. Carefully glue the triangles to the convex sides (the outwardly curved sides) of the plates.

7. Cut 6" lengths of fishing line and tape the ends to the top edges of the plates.

Hammer It Home

Review the story of Jesus' birth. Remind children that even though Jesus was laid in a simple manger, He is God's Son who was sent to love and save them. Tell them to hang these special suncatchers in their windows to remind them of Jesus' great love all year long.

14

Nature wrist wraps

10 min.

Pre-K

Grab Your Gear:
- double-sided tape
- small dried flowers, petals, and leaves
- glitter (in various colors)
- empty toilet tissue or paper towel tubes
- scissors
- hairspray (optional)

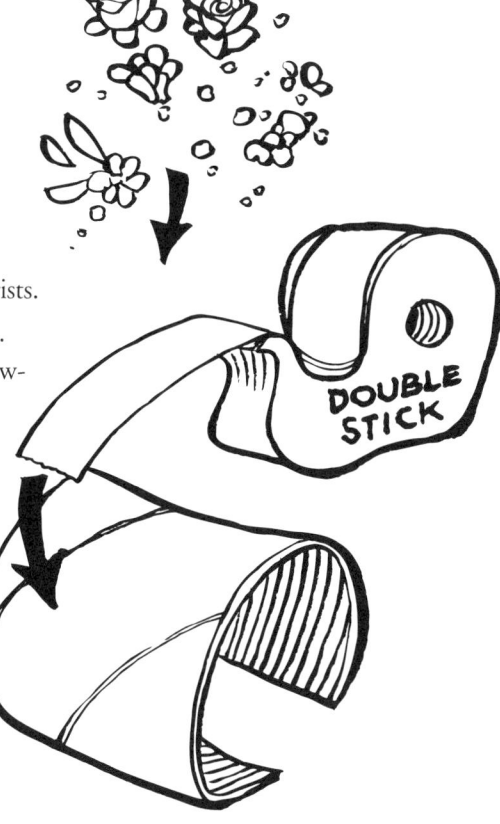

Note: If you have time to let children take a walk around the yard, they can substitute real flowers and leaves for dried ones.

Get to Work:
1. Cut toilet tissue tubes into segments 2" wide, one segment per person. Then cut one side of each segment to make the tubes slip easily onto wrists.
2. Hide dried flowers and leaves in easy-to-find places around the room. (Omit this step if you plan to go outside on a nature walk to find flowers and leaves.)
3. Stick double-sided tape to the outside of the tubes. Slip the tubes on children's wrists.
4. Go on a walk (indoors or out), finding tiny flowers, petals, and leaves and sticking them on the wrist wraps.
5. Once the wrist wraps have a variety of flowers and leaves stuck to them, sprinkle glitter on the remaining areas of exposed tape.
6. Spray the wrist wraps with hairspray (if desired) to give a thin protective coating.

Hammer It Home

After collecting the flowers and leaves on the wrist wraps, invite children to show and tell about their lovely bracelets. Then ask them who made the flowers, leaves, and the whole world. Remind children that God has given them many wonderful gifts because of His great love—including the greatest gift of all: Jesus!

Measure Up and Obey!

15 min.

Grab Your Gear:
- bright yellow electrical tape
- yellow ribbon (3" wide; 2' per child)
- fine-tipped permanent black markers
- small self-adhesive numbers
- small pill bottles or film canisters with lids (1 per child)
- heart- or star-shaped stickers

Get to Work:
1. Before class, cut a 2' length of ribbon for each child.
2. Using the permanent markers, make 20 slashes down each ribbon (like marks on a measuring tape, but at about 1½" intervals).
3. Stick numbers to the ribbons, beginning at one end with the number 1 and proceeding up to 20.
4. Using yellow electrical tape, cover the small bottles. (Do not attach lids yet.)
5. Decorate the bottles using stickers.
6. Tape the ends of the measuring ribbons (by the number 20) to the inside edges of the bottles. Stuff the ribbons into the bottles and snap on the lids. (If you're worried about children swallowing the lids, simply discard them.)

Hammer It Home

Have children pull out their measuring ribbons and pretend to measure items around the room. As they do so, count with them as they point to the numbers. Explain that when they count, the numbers always go in the same order—each number knows which number to follow. Tell children that obeying God means following Him and doing what He wants them to do. Remind them to obey their parents and teachers too, because that also makes God very happy.

Have children spread out around the room and place their ribbons on the floor. Then lead them in this action rhyme as they hop beside their measuring ribbons.

Pre-K

We can hop—1, 2

(Hop to the numbers 1 and 2.)

And obey God in all we do!

(Sway back and forth in place.)

We can hop—3, 4

(Hop to the numbers 3 and 4.)

And obey God more and more!

(Sway back and forth in place.)

We can hop to number 5

(Hop to number 5.)

And obey God all our lives!

(Sway back and forth in place.)

For a fun variation, invite a child to call out a number; then have everyone hop to that number on their measuring ribbons. Help children store the ribbons in their bottles when they're finished playing.

Sweet-Scent Necklaces

20 min.

Grab Your Gear:
- large colored or striped paper clips (24 per child)
- powdered fruit drink mixes (strawberry, cherry, orange, and grape)
- markers
- hole punch
- white card stock
- satin cord (optional)
- scissors
- white craft glue
- fruit patterns from page 19
- photocopier

Note: If children are very young and you're worried about a chain made from paper clips, substitute 18" lengths of satin cord and thread the fruit pieces directly onto the cord.

Get to Work:
1. Photocopy sets of paper fruits onto white card stock (one set per child). Cut out the pieces.
2. Give each child a set of fruit ovals and talk about each type of fruit. Have children color their fruit shapes as follows: red for the strawberries, pink for the cherries, orange for the oranges, and purple for the grapes.
3. Spread a thin layer of glue over the front of each oval.
4. While the glue is still wet and sticky, sprinkle the appropriate powdered drink mix over the glue. Gently blow on the glue to speed drying time.
5. Punch a hole at the top of each fruit oval and string the ovals onto paper clips, one fruit per clip. (Or string satin cord through the holes.)
6. If you're using paper clips, hook them together in a chain. (Each chain will need about 20 clips.) Then hook the first and last clips together. Hook the fruits on the paper clips onto the chain. (Or if you're using satin cord, tie the ends together after stringing on the paper fruit.) When the glue is completely dry, scratch the fruit pieces to release the sweet scents.

Hammer It Home

Ask children to name things that smell good (such as flowers, hot chocolate, or warm bread). Point out that good scents make us feel happy. Remind children that when they obey God, it makes Him feel happy too. As children point to each fruit on their necklaces, let them name one way they can obey God (being kind, sharing, praying, helping, etc.).

Pre-K

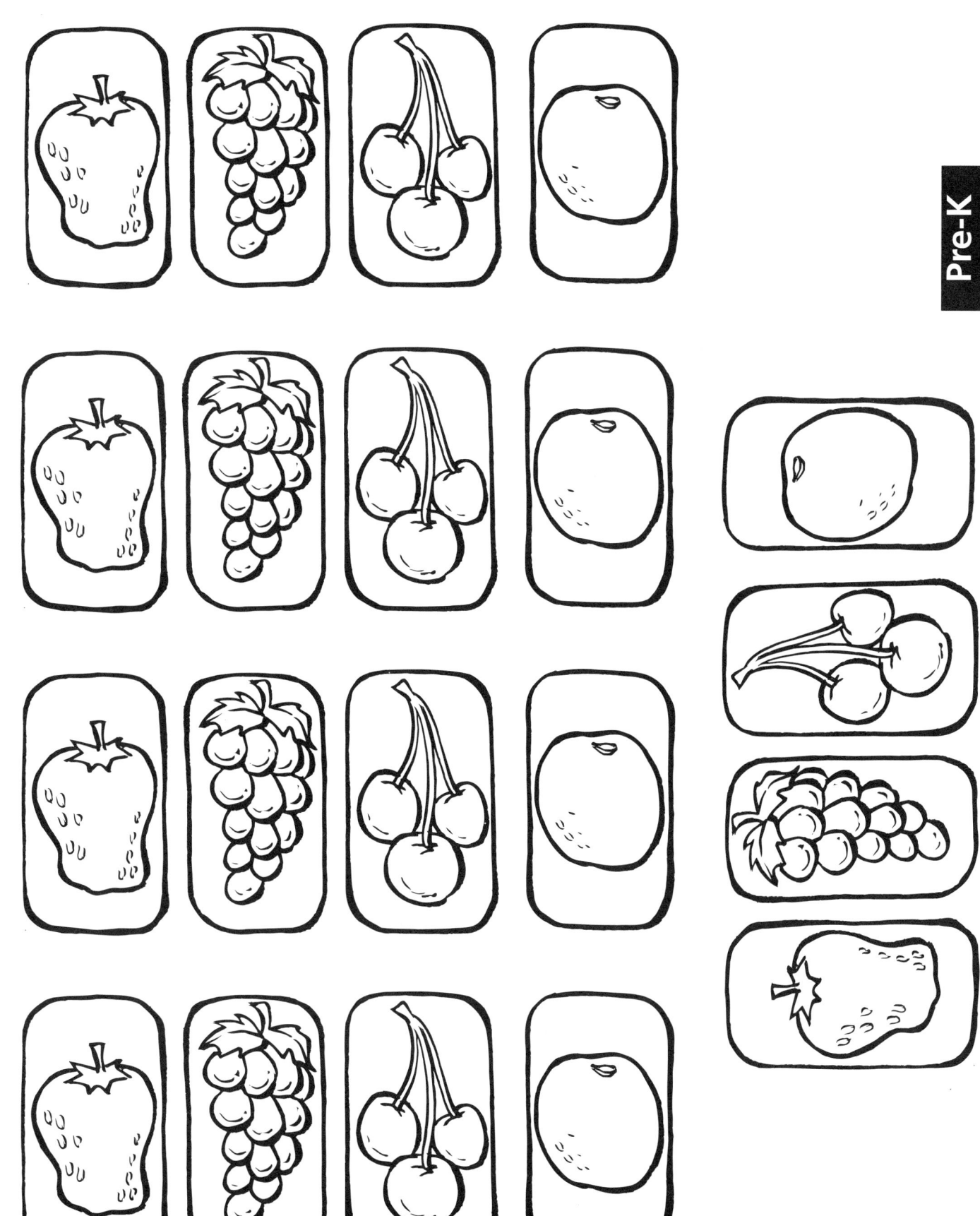

19

Flower-Print Doilies

20 min.

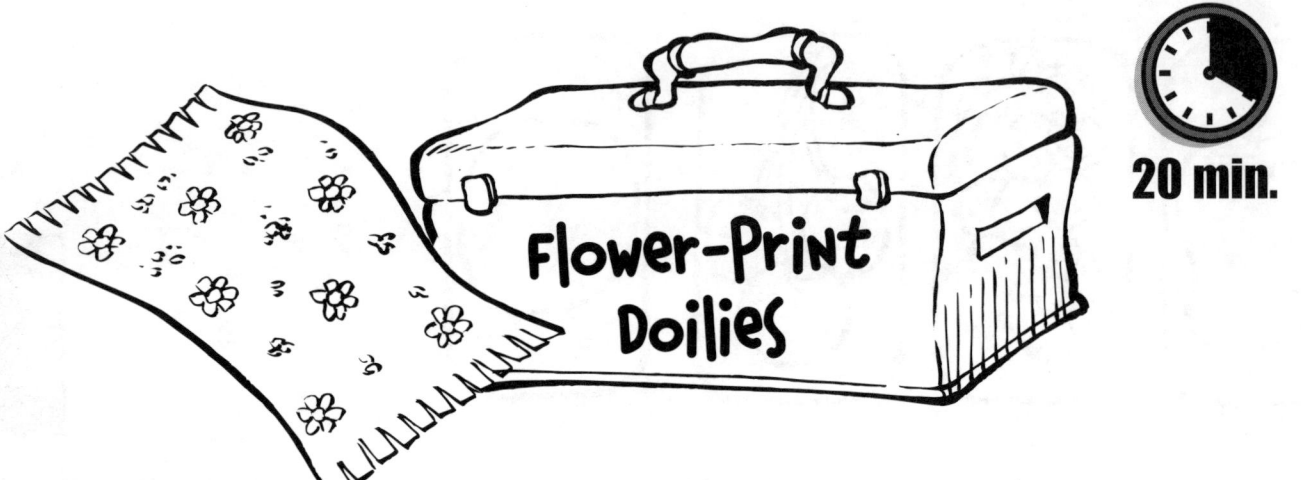

Grab Your Gear:
- 2' squares of white cotton fabric (1 per child)
- scissors
- glue
- small hammers
- fresh leaves and flowers (dandelions, geraniums, and petunias work well)
- craft foam (or precut foam flower shapes)
- small wooden blocks
- tempera paints
- paper plates
- iron (optional, but helpful)

Get to Work:

1. Before class, prepare several flower stampers by gluing craft-foam flowers on small wooden blocks.
2. Give each child a square of white cotton. Lay the fabric square on a hard surface such as a tile or wooden floor or a sidewalk. Then place several flowers, petals, or leaves on one half of the fabric square. Fold the other half over the items.
3. Use small hammers to gently pound the flowers and leaves inside the cloth folds. (The natural colors from the petals and leaves will leave pretty designs when the fabric is opened!) Remove the flattened flowers and leaves, and add new ones until you have a pleasing design. (Iron the cloths at this point if desired.)
4. Pour small amounts of tempera paints on paper plates and use the flower stampers to make colorful prints on the cloths.
5. After the cloths dry for several minutes, use scissors to slightly fringe the edges of the cloth squares.

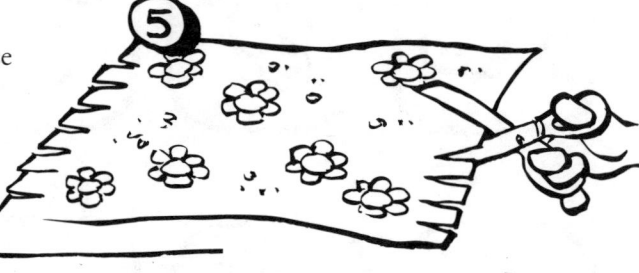

Hammer It Home

Remind children that flowers come up every year. Point out that God made flowers to faithfully bloom each year in the spring, summer, and fall to give us beauty and enjoyment. Tell children that when they continually do something such as praying to God or thanking Him, it shows they're faithful. Tell children to place their pretty doilies under lamps or bowls on their tables at home as reminders to be faithful to God.

Rainbows and Promises

10 min.

Pre-K

Grab Your Gear:
- paper plates (cut in half; 1 half per child)
- 2" construction paper squares (red, orange, yellow, green, blue, and purple; 1 square of each color per child)
- tacky craft glue
- scissors
- tinsel or aluminum foil
- cotton balls
- ribbon (8" per child)
- clear tape

Note: If you choose to use aluminum foil, cut the foil into 1" x 10" strips, 10 per child.

Get to Work:

1. Give each child a paper plate half and six paper squares (one of each color).

2. Glue the squares in the following order to the curved edge of a paper plate: red, orange, yellow, green, blue, and purple. (You may have to overlap the squares slightly, depending on the size of your paper plates.) Make a game out of finding each color and gluing it in place, beginning at the left side of the paper plate edge. The colored squares will form a rainbow.

3. When the colored squares are in place, glue tinsel or aluminum foil strips along the straight edges of the paper plate halves. This will be the rain.

4. After the rain is in place, glue cotton ball clouds to the area on the plates between the rain and the rainbow. (Older children may enjoy learning how to gently stretch the cotton balls into interesting cloud shapes.)

5. Cut 8" pieces of ribbon and tape the ends to the tops of the plates, making hanging loops. These loops can slide over small wrists or be used to hang the projects on windows or walls.

Hammer It Home

Have children identify each color on their rainbows. Tell them that God made rainbows as a sign of His promise to love them and keep them safe. Explain that they can be faithful to God by always keeping their promises too! Then have children skip around with their rainbows, singing the following song to the tune of "Row, Row, Row Your Boat."

Faith, faith, faith, and love,
Rainbows great and small—
Faith and love from God above
Will shower on us all.

This Little Light

Grab Your Gear:
- wide craft sticks (1 per child)
- colored markers
- tacky craft glue
- scissors
- yellow or orange glitter glue
- hinge-style clothespins (1 per child)
- self-adhesive magnetic tape
- flame and "Faith Holds On!" patterns from page 23
- stiff white paper
- photocopier

Get to Work:

1. Photocopy on stiff white paper the patterns for the flame and slogan on page 23. Cut out a flame and slogan strip for each child. (Or consider making the flames and glow circles using brightly colored craft foam.)
2. Use markers to color a craft stick.
3. Give each child a flame design. Color the flames orange and red; color the "glow" around them yellow.
4. Glue the circles to the tops of the craft sticks.
5. Color the hinge-style clothespins. Then glue the clothespins to the backs of the craft sticks, with the hinged "mouths" of the pins pointing toward the bottoms of the sticks.
6. Snip a half-inch piece of self-adhesive magnetic tape and stick it to the back of the clothespin.
7. Glue the "Faith Holds On!" strip to the front of the craft stick. Read the slogan aloud with each child.
8. Add a bit of yellow glitter to the glow lines around the flames.

Hammer It Home

Have children stand in a circle, holding their Little Lights. Sing "This Little Light of Mine" once. Then help kids clip their candles to their shirts. Tell them that their faith in Jesus can shine like a candle when they do things that please Him. Let children name examples of ways they can let their faith shine each and every day (help a friend, go to church, etc.).

22

FAITH HOLDS ON!

FAITH HOLDS ON!

FAITH HOLDS ON!

FAITH HOLDS ON!

FAITH HOLDS ON!

Hairy Helpers

10 min.

Grab Your Gear:
- polar fleece (a variety of colors and patterns)
- wide craft sticks (pre-colored if possible)
- markers
- rubber bands
- googly eyes
- tacky craft glue
- scissors

Get to Work:
1. Before class, cut the polar fleece into 1" x 10" strips (6–10 per person).
2. Use markers to color the wide craft sticks if they aren't pre-colored. Patchwork designs or stripes work nicely.
3. Choose several strips of polar fleece. Double the strips over end-to-end and hold them in a bundle.
4. Slide the ends of the craft sticks into the middle of the polar fleece bundle. Securely attach the ends of the strips to the end of the stick using a rubber band. (The fleece loops will make floppy "hair.")
5. Glue googly eyes to the craft stick and add a smiling mouth using markers.

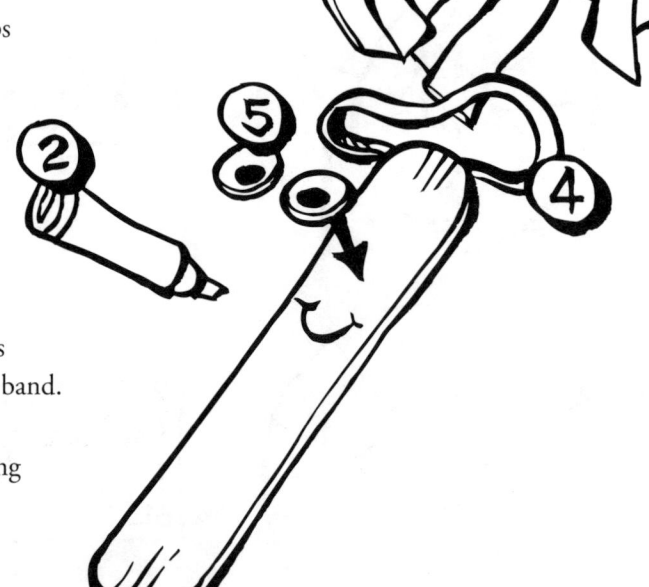

Hammer It Home

Ask children to name different tools and tell about their uses. Be sure to include tools that help around the house such as dusters, sponges, vacuum cleaners, brooms, and mops. Tell children that their Hairy Helpers love to help and clean. Then challenge them to use their Hairy Helper "tools" to help build good feelings in their families by dusting tables and shelves.

Your preschoolers and kindergartners will enjoy this lively action song using their new Hairy Helpers! Tell children that Hairy Helper loves to help and he loves to clean too. Then lead them in happily shaking their dusters and singing the following song to the tune of "Old MacDonald."

Pre-K

I can show God that I care

Dust, dust, dust, dust, dust

(Shake dusters high.)

By helping others here and there

Dust, dust, dust, dust, dust

(Shake dusters to sides.)

With a dust up here and a dust down there

(Shake dusters high, then low.)

Here a dust, there a dust, everywhere a dust, dust

(Hold dusters and twirl around.)

I can show God that I care

(Shake dusters high.)

Dust, dust, dust, dust, dust

(Shake dusters to sides.)

Nest Nibblers

15 min.

Grab Your Gear:
- paint stir sticks (1 per child)
- peanut butter
- birdseed and unsalted sunflower seeds
- plastic knives
- paper grocery sacks
- twine or string (3' per student)
- scissors
- crepe paper
- ribbon
- duct tape (optional)

Get to Work:

1. Give each child a stir stick. Use a plastic knife to spread peanut butter on both sides of each stick, leaving empty a one-inch strip at each end.
2. Pour birdseed and unsalted sunflower seeds in paper grocery sacks. Drop the paint stick in a sack and shake it until the stick is covered with seeds.
3. Tie a 3' length of twine or string to the ends of the paint stick.
4. Cut varying lengths of crepe paper and ribbon (4–10"). Loosely tie or tape the crepe paper strips across the length of the twine or string. (Birds and squirrels will love the brightly colored paper and will put it to use in building their nests!)
5. Tell children to hang their Nest Nibblers on trees, shrubs, or fences by looping the strings over branches or posts. (Children might enjoy making a second project to give away to a friend, grandparent, or neighbor.)

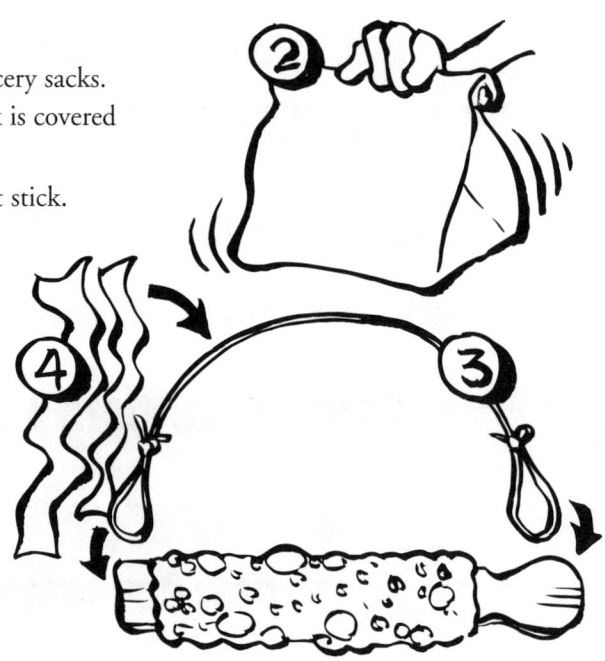

Hammer It Home

Talk about different ways God cares for birds and squirrels, giving them food, water, nests, and warm fur. Point out that God cares for your students, just as He cares for all of nature. Ask children to talk about ways God cares for them and ways they can show His love by caring for others.

I'm Loved Banners

15 min.

Grab Your Gear:
- paint stir sticks (2 per child)
- tacky craft glue
- scissors
- colored, self-adhesive craft foam circles (6" in diameter)
- permanent markers
- googly eyes
- curly doll hair (in various colors)
- duct tape
- satin cord or ribbon
- craft foam sheets (1 per child)
- 1" self-adhesive letters (optional)

Get to Work:

1. Before class, cut sheets of craft foam into rectangles that are 10" high and as wide as the length of your stir sticks. Cut the 6" circles in half, one half per person.
2. Glue paint stir sticks along the top and bottom edges of the foam rectangles using tacky craft glue.
3. Glue the half-circles to the bottom center of the foam rectangles, along the top edge of the lower stir sticks. (See illustration.) Glue on googly eyes and draw smiles on the half-circles using markers. Glue curly hair to the top edges of the half-circles.
4. Use markers (or self-adhesive letters) to write the following phrase at the top of each banner: *Jesus Loves (child's name)!*
5. Make a hanger by cutting a 16" length of satin cord or ribbon and duct taping the ends to the back of the banner.

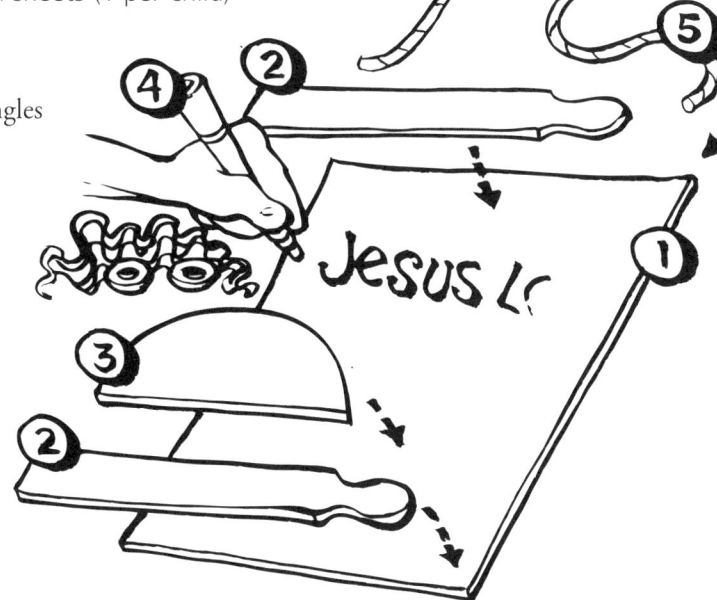

Hammer It Home

Remind children that because Jesus loves them so greatly, He forgives the wrong things they say and do. Explain that if they love Jesus, they should be willing to forgive others. If time allows, play a quick game of "Who Does Jesus Love?" Ask the question; then choose a child to hold his banner high and say, "Jesus loves (name)!" Repeat the game but this time ask, "Who does Jesus forgive?" Let each child answer by holding her banner high and saying, "Jesus forgives (name)!"

Magnetic Puzzle

15 min.

Grab Your Gear:
- self-adhesive magnetic tape
- scissors
- white card stock
- crayons
- zip-top baggies (one per child)
- "Jesus Loves Me" art from page 29
- photocopier

Get to Work:

1. Before class, copy the "Jesus Loves Me" art from page 29 onto white card stock (one copy per child).
2. Color the pictures as desired using crayons.
3. Cut each picture into various puzzle shapes.
4. Attach a piece of magnetic tape to each puzzle piece.
5. Store each set of puzzle pieces in a zip-top bag.

Hammer It Home

Let children play with their puzzles as time allows. Read aloud the phrase on the artwork and help children practice saying those words together several times. Tell them that they can put these puzzles on refrigerator doors or file cabinets at home. Remind children that, because Jesus loves them so much, He forgives every wrong thing they do, and that they should try every day to be forgiving like Jesus.

28

JESUS LOVES ME

PRIMARY MIDDLER

Primaries
- Need to know they are loved and supported by the teacher.
- Enjoy the freedom of working independently.
- Need honest praise, encouragement, and opportunities for success.
- Are happiest when participating in a purposeful activity (in which they know the "hows" and "whys").
- Want challenging activities but have not yet developed fine-muscle coordination.

Middlers
- Are developing physically at a steady, but slow, pace.
- Are curious explorers and want to know why they are doing something.
- Want to be allowed to express themselves.
- Are searching for self-identity but still respond to gentle guidance and encouragement from adults.

So...
- Show a finished sample of the activity or project. Give thorough instructions.
- Give help as needed but allow as much self-expression as possible.
- Be prepared for some good-natured rowdiness.
- Provide clean-up materials and have the students clean up on their own as much as possible.
- Have other activities or projects planned for those who finish quickly. This helps to allay any possible discipline problems ahead of time.

Measuring Tape Belts

20 min.

Grab Your Gear:
- rolls of belt webbing (1" wide, available at fabric stores; approximately 30" per child)
- slide-tooth buckle sets (available at fabric stores)
- black permanent fabric markers
- glitter glue in squeeze bottles
- small number stickers (optional)
- fabric glue
- yardsticks
- plastic jewels, flat washers, shiny pennies (optional)

Note: Small number stickers for calendars can be found at hobby or office supply stores. These stickers work well for numbering the belts when held in place with fabric glue. If you choose not to use these stickers, use black fabric pens to write the numbers. Belt buckle sets come with the buckle and a saw-tooth tip for the opposite end of the belt.

Get to Work:

1. Let each child wrap belt webbing (from the roll) around her waist. Cut the webbing 3" longer.

2. Using yardsticks and permanent fabric markers, mark inches and half-inches on the belt webbing, beginning at the far left end and moving to the right end. (Make sure the marks are dark enough to see plainly.)

3. Using either small number stickers (which should be glued on with fabric glue) or permanent fabric markers, number the belts along the inch marks, working from left to right.

4. Distribute the buckle sets. Position the belt end pieces at the left end of the webbing (beside the number 1). Squeeze the end pieces tightly by hand to secure the saw-tooth clamps.

5. Lay out the belts and trace the inch and half-inch lines with glitter glue pens.

6. Squeeze a thin layer of glitter glue over the belt buckle and stick on plastic jewels, flat metal washers, or shiny pennies as decorations if desired. Let the belts dry.

Hammer It Home

Invite children to tell how measuring tapes, rulers, and yardsticks are used in building projects. Then explain that character qualities like humility, obedience, faithfulness, caring, and forgiveness can help measure their relationships with God. Tell them to wear their belts as reminders to build their lives as God desires—just like Jesus.

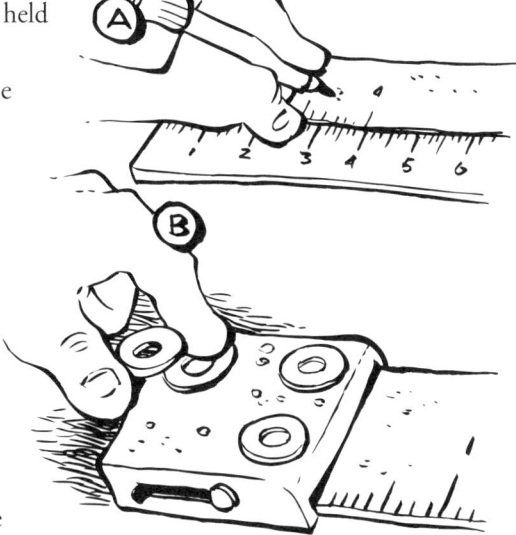

Tools of the Trade

20 min.

Grab Your Gear:
- colored construction paper
- clear tape
- scissors
- large-head screws and nails (several inches long)
- large metal washers
- markers
- white craft glue or glue sticks
- curling ribbon (in a variety of colors)
- fishing line
- tissue paper
- staplers
- tool patterns from page 35
- photocopier

Note: Before class, photocopy on colored paper a set of tools and two toolboxes for each person. (Use several different colors.) Dull the nails and screws by rubbing the tips on concrete.

Get to Work:

1. Give each child two paper toolbox patterns. Cut out the toolboxes along the dotted lines and then tape or staple the two patterns together (print sides out) along the tops and sides, leaving the bottom edges open.
2. Use tissue paper to stuff the paper toolboxes. Staple or tape the bottoms and sides closed.
3. Cut varying lengths of colored curling ribbon and curl it using scissors. Then tape the curls along the bottom edge of the toolbox.
4. Give each person a set of colored paper tools. Cut out the tools along the outside lines.
5. Briefly talk with children about the words written on each tool and their meanings.
6. On the back of each tool, let children list ways they could put that characteristic into practice.
7. Cut varying lengths of fishing line and tape one end of each piece to the top of a tool. Then tape the loose ends of the line to the bottom of the toolbox.
8. Cut several more lengths of fishing line or ribbon and tie them around washers, nails, and screws. Tape the loose ends of the line to the bottom of the toolbox. Then cut a 10" length of fishing line and tape it in a loop to the top of each toolbox for hanging.

Hammer It Home

Have children hold up their toolboxes. Explain that the phrase, "tools of the trade" means having the right tools to get the job done. Tell children that their job is to build their lives and hearts like Jesus and that God has given them these tools to make that happen. Challenge children to hang their toolboxes where they'll be reminded often about the importance of building their lives like Christ.

Tools For Building Strong Lives in God!

- OBEDIENCE
- CARING
- FAITHFULNESS
- HUMILITY
- FORGIVENESS

Tool Aprons

25 min.

Grab Your Gear:

- small, canvas tool-belt aprons (available at most craft stores; use waist-tie aprons if possible)
- acrylic paints (in squeeze bottles)
- metal or plastic key chain clips (available at most craft stores; 1 or 2 per child)
- thread
- needles
- scissors
- variety of toy tools or small real tools (wrenches, screw drivers, hammers, etc., one or two per person)
- glitter glue (in squeeze bottles)
- orange or red plastic gems (for Darrel's light; 1 per child)
- tacky craft glue
- iron
- ironing board
- iron-on transfer paper
- pattern of Darrel from page 37
- photocopier or computer with printer and scanner

Note: Before class, copy the Darrel pattern from page 37 onto iron-on transfer paper. You can do this by photocopying the pattern onto the transfer paper or by scanning the pattern onto a computer and printing it out on the transfer paper. See manufacturer's instructions for more details. Prepare one transfer per child. To save time, transfer the pictures to the aprons before class. (A less expensive, but more time-consuming, option is an iron-on transfer pen, available at craft stores. Follow manufacturer's instructions.)

Get to Work:

1. Give each child an apron with a transfer on one of the pockets.
2. Carefully sew one or two key chain clips onto the waistband of the apron. (Children may omit the clips if they wish or if they're too young to sew.)
3. Color and decorate the Darrel image using bright paints and glitter.
4. Glue an orange or red gem on the apron for Darrel's light.
5. On one of the pockets without the transfer, use fabric paints to write the words *Build with care!* If there are other empty pockets on the aprons, add the words *Build with love!* Embellish these pockets with paint or glitter as desired. Set the aprons aside to dry.
6. Give each person one or two tools to decorate with permanent markers and paint. Children may use stripes, swirls, or other simple designs to add whimsy and fun to the tools.
7. When the aprons and tools are dry, slide the tools into the pockets.

Hammer It Home

Help children tie their aprons around their waists. Briefly talk about each tool and why it is important for builders to keep their tools handy. Ask children to name tools that might be important for them as they build their lives for God (prayer, Bibles, family, etc.). Remind them to keep those tools handy and use them often!

Pri-Mid

37

Switch Plate Scenes

15 min.

Grab Your Gear:
- craft sticks (11 per child)
- white glue
- scissors
- corrugated cardboard
- double-sided tape
- crayons or markers
- artwork for add-ons from page 39
- photocopier

Get to Work:

1. Before class, copy the artwork for the add-on pieces from page 39 (one set per child).
2. Use glue to mount the add-on pieces on corrugated cardboard. Trim pieces and allow to dry.
3. Use crayons or markers to color eleven craft sticks as desired.
4. Using the illustration on page 39 as a guide, make a switch plate cover from craft sticks and glue. You will need to gently break one of the craft sticks to allow for the light switch. (See illustration.) Allow glue to dry.
5. When the add-on pieces are dry, choose the desired artwork and color with crayons or markers.
6. Glue the add-ons to the switch plate as desired.
7. Apply strips of double-sided tape to the back of each switch plate. The tape will adhere the plate to the existing light switch cover.

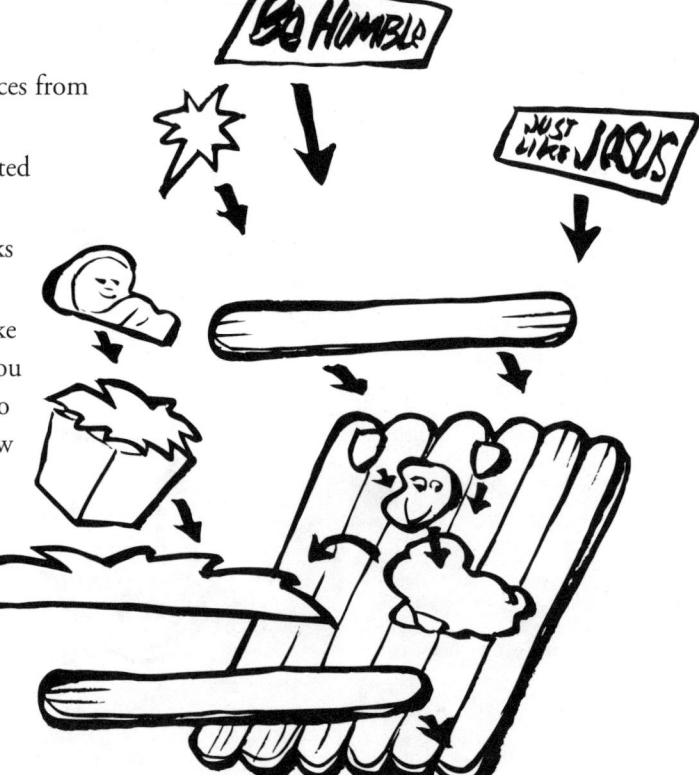

Hammer It Home

Review the story of Jesus' birth and the humble manner in which He came. Tell children that the Bible refers to Jesus as the Light of the World because He brought hope to a very sad place, just as a real light shines in the darkness. Children can put these switch plate covers in their rooms as reminders of Jesus' humble birth and as a constant challenge to "shine" His love to others.

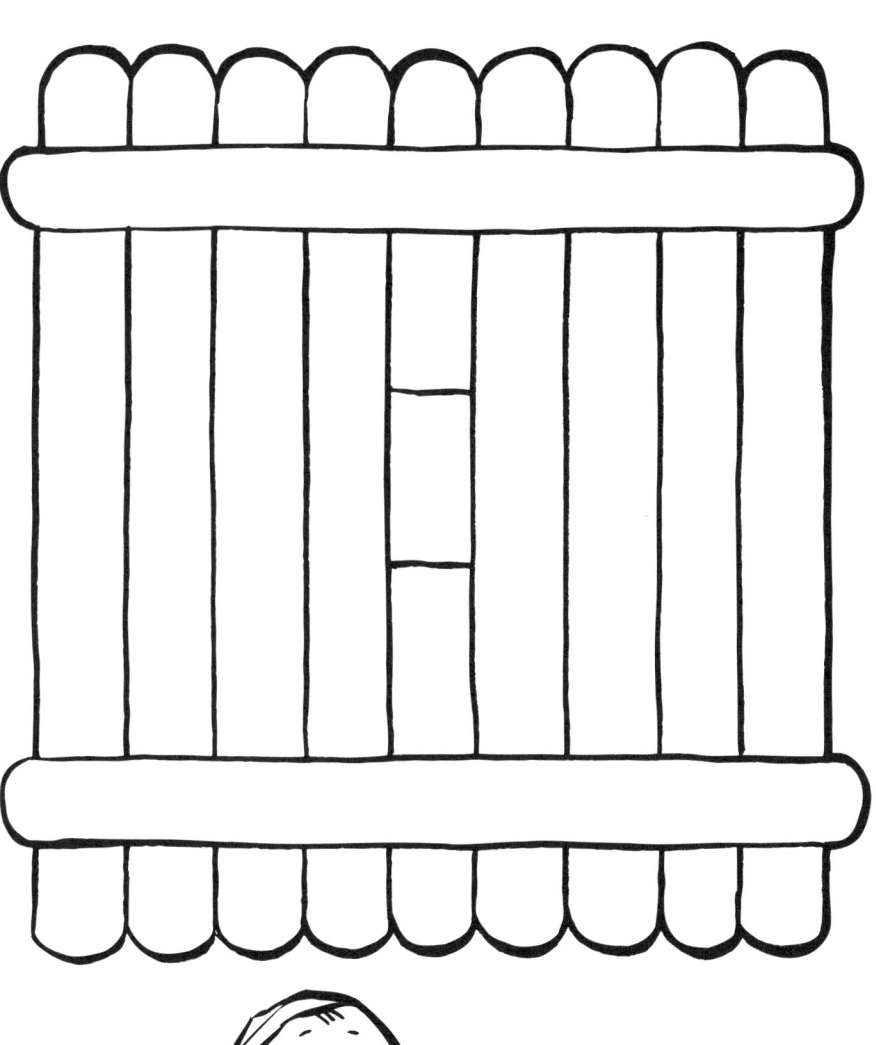

Be Humble

Just Like Jesus

Pri–Mid

39

Humble Lanterns

25 min.

Grab Your Gear:
- craft sticks (16 per child; pre-colored sticks will save time)
- self-adhesive craft foam hearts or red tissue paper
- scissors
- glue sticks
- tacky craft glue
- brightly colored markers or tempera paints and brushes (if the craft sticks are not colored)
- sheets of craft foam
- fine-tipped permanent markers
- wax paper (a 24" length for each child)
- tea light candles (1 per child)
- blow-dryers (optional)

Note: For each child, cut a square of craft foam that is as wide and long as the craft sticks you're using. These squares will be the bottoms of the lanterns.

Get to Work:

1. Distribute the craft sticks. If the sticks aren't already colored, color them using markers or tempera paints. Then give each person a length of wax paper. Lay the wax paper on a table. Beginning at the left side of the paper, glue down four sticks in the shape of a square. (The sticks should not overlap, but should touch at the tips. Make sure the colored sides are facing upward.) Directly beside the first square (to the right), glue four more sticks into the shape of another square. Repeat these steps two more times until there are a total of four side-by-side squares.

2. Give each person four self-adhesive craft foam hearts. Remove the backings and place one heart in the center of each square. (If you're using red tissue paper, cut out four hearts and glue them in the centers of the squares.)

3. Allow the squares to dry for at least 10 minutes or use blow-dryers to speed up the drying time. When the glue is dry, trim the wax paper along the top of the row of squares. Also trim along the sides, leaving ½" of wax paper at one end, forming a tab. Then trim along the bottom edge of the squares. Form a box, keeping the hearts on the outside. Glue the wax paper tab to the neighboring craft stick to secure the box. Glue craft foam squares to the bottoms of the lanterns and allow to dry for several minutes. Place tea lights inside.

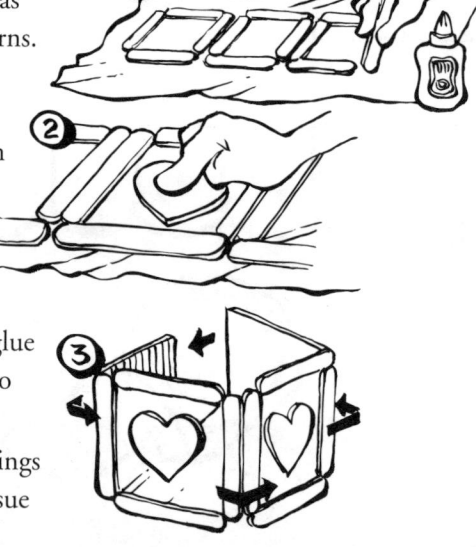

Hammer It Home

Explain that even a candle's gentle flame shines brightly in the darkness. Talk about how Jesus came to earth as a humble baby to light the way for us. Challenge children to place their Humble Lanterns on their tables at home and ask adults to light them at mealtime. Children can remind their families about being humble as Jesus was and talk about ways to shine their own lights in a dark world.

Juggling Sticks

20 min.

Grab Your Gear:
- ⅝" x 18" dowel rods (1 per child)
- ⅜" x 12" dowel rods (1 per child)
- rolls of colored electrical tape (in several colors)
- duct tape
- colorful felt or craft foam
- tacky craft glue
- scissors
- pencils
- tape measures

Get to Work:

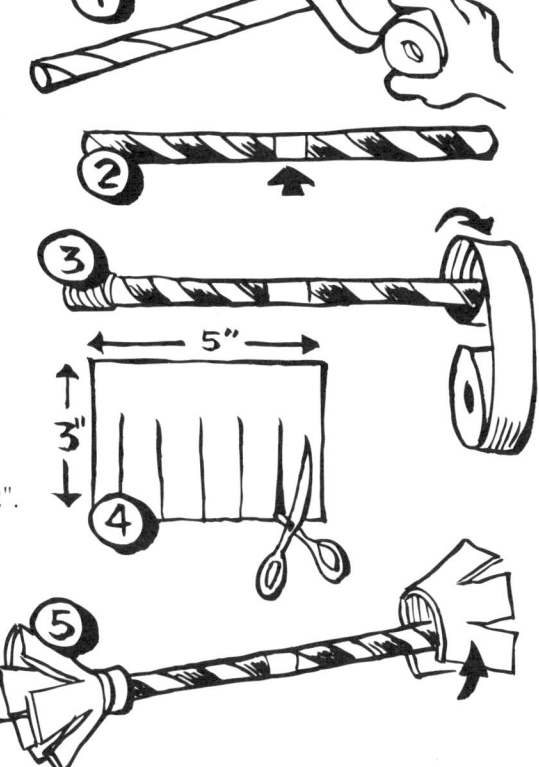

1. Give each child a large and small dowel rod. Wrap colored tape down each dowel to make interesting stripes.

2. Use a tape measure and pencil to mark the center of each dowel. Then identify this point by wrapping one color of tape around the rod several times.

3. Wrap duct tape on both ends of each stick in equal amounts (for even weight distribution, approximately ½" thick on each end). Check the weight by balancing the stick on your fingertip at its center point.

4. Cut colorful felt or craft foam into two 3" x 5" rectangles. Then fringe the rectangles along one side, cutting in about 2".

5. Wrap the uncut sides of the fringed rectangles around the ends of the sticks and tape them in place with colored electrical tape. The ends of the juggling sticks should have almost a pom-pom look to them. (If you want bigger ends, simply cut several fringed rectangles and tape them in place on the ends of the sticks.)

Hammer It Home

Let children try to balance their Juggling Sticks on their wrists, fingers, noses, or heads. Then see if they can twirl the sticks and toss them as if they're juggling (best suited for outdoors!). Invite children to talk about why juggling more than one thing is hard, and then to give examples of things in their lives that they try to "juggle" (school, friends, sports, church, etc.). Tell them that when they put God first in their lives and obey His will, He will help them balance everything else.

41

Scripture Clips

20 min.

Grab Your Gear:
- wooden mouse traps (1 per child)
- pliers
- tempera paints
- paintbrushes
- bowls of water
- newspaper
- star and heart stickers
- permanent markers or small, self-adhesive letters
- glitter glue
- tacky craft glue
- small plastic jewels
- self-adhesive magnetic tape (4" per child)
- scissors
- colored construction paper
- verse card patterns from page 43
- photocopier

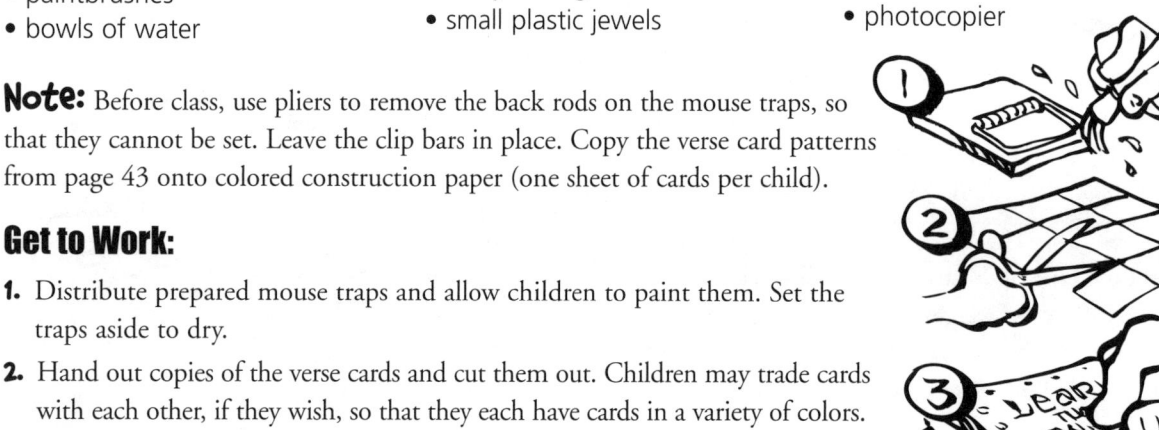

Note: Before class, use pliers to remove the back rods on the mouse traps, so that they cannot be set. Leave the clip bars in place. Copy the verse card patterns from page 43 onto colored construction paper (one sheet of cards per child).

Get to Work:

1. Distribute prepared mouse traps and allow children to paint them. Set the traps aside to dry.
2. Hand out copies of the verse cards and cut them out. Children may trade cards with each other, if they wish, so that they each have cards in a variety of colors.
3. When the mouse traps are dry, lay them on a table with the clips pointing downward. On the top portions of the traps, use permanent markers or self-adhesive letters to spell out the words *Learn the Word!*
4. Embellish the traps with stickers, glitter glue, or plastic jewels.
5. Stick two 2" pieces of magnetic tape to the back of each mouse trap. Carefully lift the clips and slide the Scripture cards under them. Tell children to work on memorizing one verse for a week, and then place a new card on top until they've memorized all 12 verses!

Hammer It Home

Talk about how Jesus went to the temple as a young boy and was found teaching with wisdom and authority. Ask students why they think Jesus wanted to teach others about God. Talk about why children should also want to learn and use God's Word and how it will help them as they build their lives daily for Him. Challenge children to place their Scripture Clips on their refrigerators and invite their families to learn God's Word along with them!

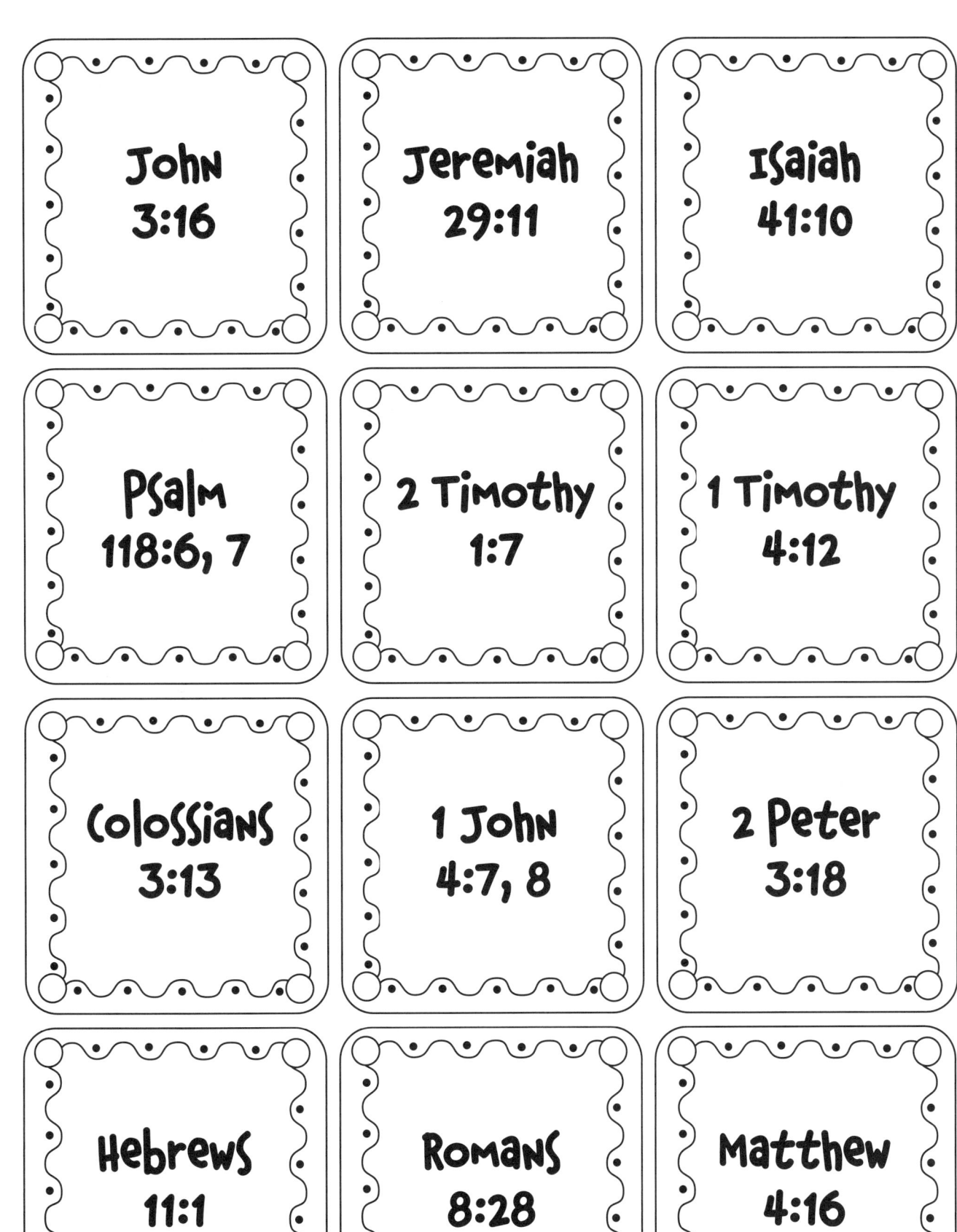

John 3:16	Jeremiah 29:11	Isaiah 41:10
Psalm 118:6, 7	2 Timothy 1:7	1 Timothy 4:12
Colossians 3:13	1 John 4:7, 8	2 Peter 3:18
Hebrews 11:1	Romans 8:28	Matthew 4:16

Pri–Mid

Decorative Doorstops

20 min.

Grab Your Gear:
- modeling or florist's clay
- red bricks with holes (1 per child)
- small craft foam or felt circles
- tacky craft glue
- florist's tape
- scissors
- flexible craft wire
- round toothpicks
- small silk flowers and leaves
- small floral butterflies, bugs, birds, or other fun "creatures" (1 per child)
- newspaper
- hot glue gun (optional)

Get to Work:

1. Cover your work surface with newspaper.
2. Give each person a brick. Fill the holes in the bricks with clay by rolling out thick "snake" shapes and sliding them into the holes. (Be sure the clay fits tightly and won't slip out.)
3. Arrange silk flowers, leaves, and other decorations along the tops of the bricks. Then glue the items in place with tacky craft glue or a hot glue gun (with adult supervision). Use florist's tape to attach decorations to toothpicks, and then stick them into the clay.
4. After arranging the designs, let children help each other glue four felt or craft-foam circles to the bottom corners of the bricks. Set the bricks aside to dry.

Hammer It Home

Ask children to tell what a doorstop is and how it is used. Then point out that a doorstop keeps a door either open or closed. It can hold a door open to let in fresh air, or it can hold a door closed to keep out bugs. Remind children that they can choose what things to let into their hearts and what things to keep out. Talk with them about good things and bad things that can come into their lives, and then explain how God's Word is like a doorstop, helping them to know what things to allow in and what to keep out. Tell children to use their doorstops at home as reminders of this important lesson.

Obey and Teach Napkins

20 min.

Grab Your Gear:
- assorted dried beans (4 or more varieties)
- empty paper towel tubes (tissue or gift-wrap tubes will also work)
- tacky craft glue
- scissors
- 6" cotton fabric squares (solid colors; at least 4 squares per child)
- pinking shears
- rolls of narrow decorative trim and braids
- fabric markers
- spray sealant (optional)
- Bibles

Note: Cut the paper tubes into 1½" segments (at least four per child). Children will be making napkins and napkin rings for their families so the number of items will vary from person to person. When cutting the fabric squares, you may wish to use pinking shears to avoid ravels. Or purchase solid-colored cloth napkins or men's handkerchiefs.

Get to Work:

1. Give each child a cotton fabric square and paper tube segment for each person in his or her family. (If you're running short, place a limit of four or five squares and tell children they can share their projects or make additional ones at home.)

2. Glue dried beans to the paper tubes mosaic-style. (Try to cover the tubes completely if possible.) When all the tubes are covered in beans, set them aside to dry.

3. Using fabric markers, write the following references on the "napkins," one reference per napkin: *Luke 11:28; John 14:15; John 14:23; John 15:10; Philippians 2:8; Psalm 103:20.*

4. Use tacky craft glue to add trim to two or four sides of each napkin. Set aside to dry.

5. When the napkin rings are dry, spray them with clear sealant if you wish.

6. Roll the napkins and slide them inside the rings. Explain that these napkins and rings can be used at meals to begin discussions about obeying God and the blessings that come from doing so.

Hammer It Home

Ask volunteers to look up the Scripture references from Step 3 and read them aloud. Briefly discuss what each verse teaches about obeying God. Remind children that even as a young boy Jesus obeyed God and His parents. Challenge them to teach others about obeying God through words and actions and by sharing these special napkins with their families.

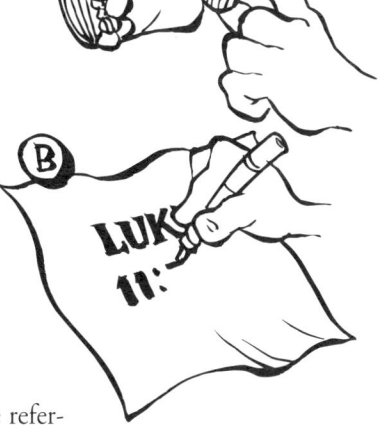

Stick-to-It Bookmarks

15 min.

Grab Your Gear:
- white card stock
- self-adhesive magnetic tape
- scissors
- clear packing tape (2" wide)
- glitter glue pens
- markers
- fine-tipped black permanent markers
- bookmark patterns from page 47
- photocopier

Note: Before class, photocopy the bookmark patterns from page 47 onto white card stock. Make one copy of the page per child, giving each a set of five bookmarks. Also cut for each child ten 1" lengths of self-adhesive magnetic tape.

Get to Work:

1. Give each child a set of bookmarks. Color the bookmarks and cut them out. Embellish with glitter glue as desired.
2. Cut five 9" lengths of clear packing tape per child and lay them on a table, sticky sides up. Carefully place a bookmark (picture side down) on one end of the tape and wrap the remaining tape over the bookmark to cover it. As you cover each bookmark, slide your hands over it to seal the tape, and then trim off any excess with scissors.
3. Fold the bookmarks in half across the centers so that the pictures are on the outsides, and then crease the bookmarks using your fingernails.
4. Remove the backing from one 1" piece of magnetic tape and stick it inside a bottom edge of one bookmark. After it is stuck, place another magnet over it. Leaving the magnets stuck together, peel the backing off the top piece and press the bookmark closed. (This will assure that the magnets are lined up properly.)

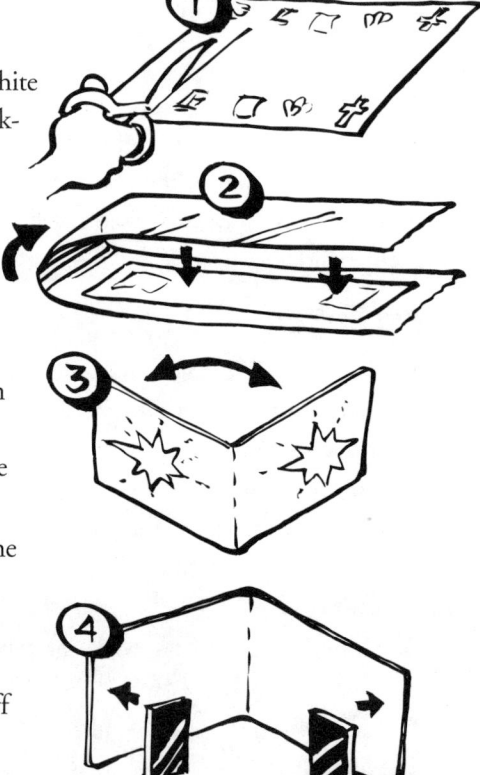

Hammer It Home

Ask children to talk about why it is important to read the Bible and why it's sometimes hard for them to do that. Remind them that even Jesus learned God's Word and used it to defeat Satan. Let children look through their Bibles and find five verses they would like to bookmark. (You may want to have some suggestions on hand, just in case.) Then have them use permanent markers to write each reference on a separate bookmark. Let each child read aloud a verse he's chosen, and then talk together about how that verse can help them build strong, faithful lives for God.

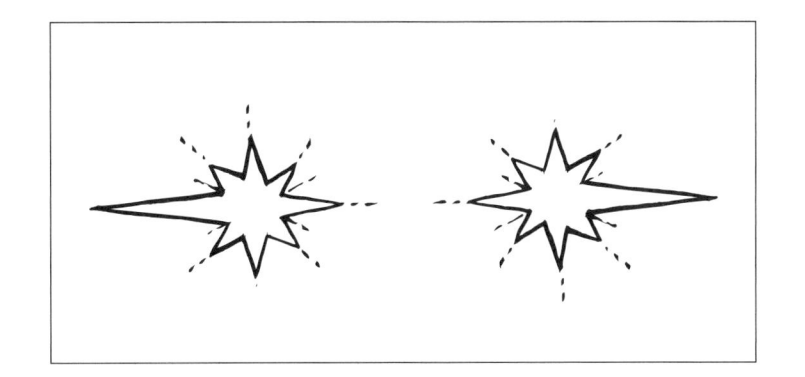

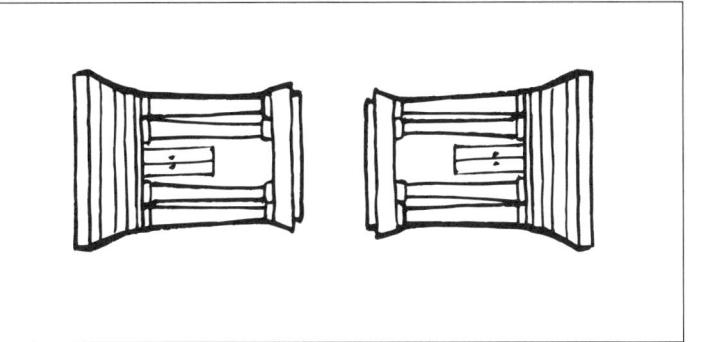

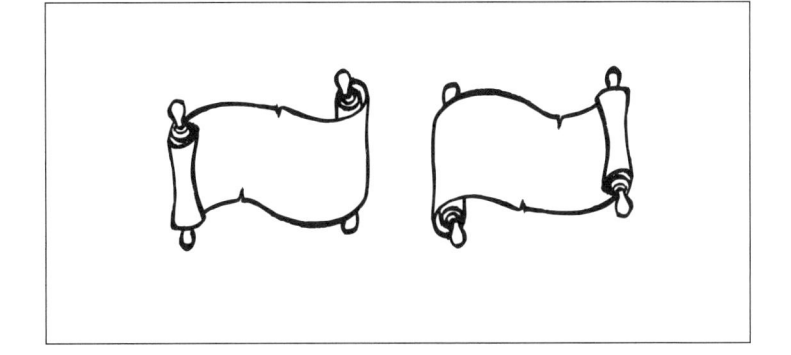

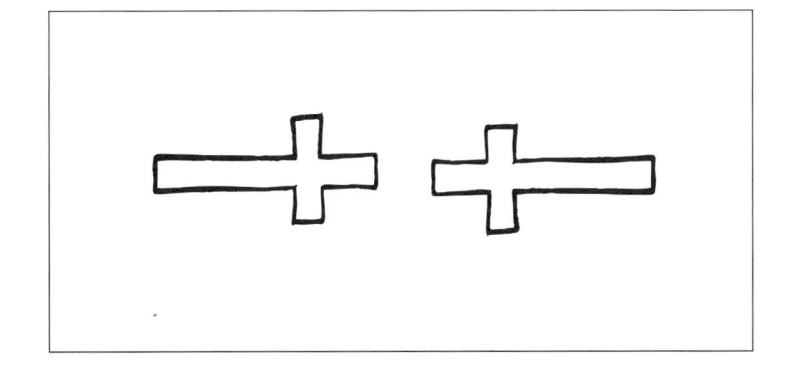

Pri–Mid

47

15 min.

Faith Wraps

Grab Your Gear:
- old, narrow leather belts (about 1" wide)
- heavy-duty scissors
- self-adhesive hook-and-loop fasteners (small circles; 1 set per child)
- several sheets of self-adhesive alphabet stickers
- tacky craft glue
- newsprint or white copy paper
- black permanent markers
- clear tape

Note: Before class, cut off the buckles and holed ends from the belts. Then cut the belts into 8" segments (one segment per child). On a sheet of paper, write the following acrostic for the word FAITH: **F**earless **A**ttitudes **I**n **T**he **H**eart. Tape the paper to a wall.

Get to Work:
1. Distribute the belt segments. Rub the belts to make them even more pliable, and then lay them on a table right side up.
2. Glue stickers to the belts, spelling out the word *FAITH*. (Tacky glue will hold the stickers in place more securely than adhesive alone.) Use permanent markers to add periods after each letter of the word.
3. Give each child a set of circle fasteners. Put both pieces together and peel the backing off one circle. Stick the pieces to the far right side of the OUTSIDE of the wristband (after the letter H). Peel the backing paper from the other circle, wrap the band around your wrist, and stick the circle in place on the INSIDE of the wristband. (See illustration.)
4. Let children wear their wristbands as you talk about the F.A.I.T.H. acronym. (See below.)

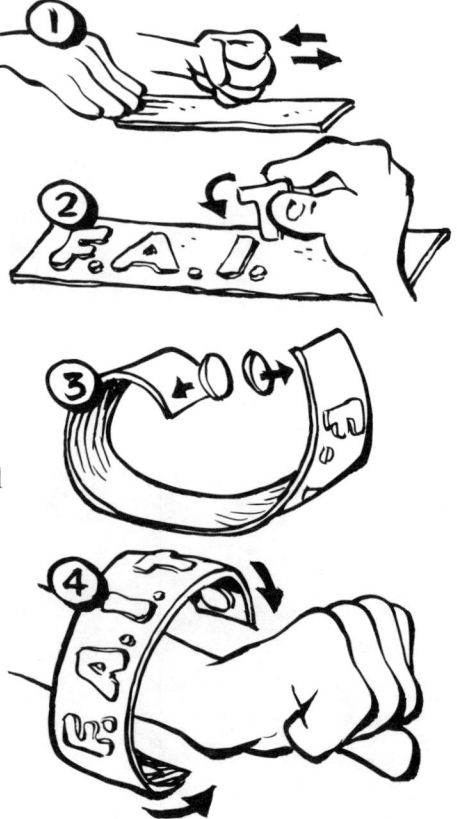

Hammer It Home

Ask a volunteer to read from the paper on the wall, explaining what the F.A.I.T.H. acronym means. Explain to children that faith in God will give them courage and strength that they might not have on their own, because they can know that He is always with them. Repeat the acronym several times, and then challenge children to wear their Faith Wraps as reminders of the power of faith.

Planning Sculptures

35 min.

Grab Your Gear:
- 8" wood bases (round or square; 1 per child)
- 2" nails with large heads (15 per child)
- thin-gauge electrical wire (in several colors)
- wire snips or sturdy scissors
- hammers
- acrylic paints
- paintbrushes
- bowls of water
- newspapers
- pencils
- colorful beads (need to fit on the electrical wire you've chosen)
- white copy paper

Get to Work:

1. Distribute white copy paper and pencils. Tell children that they'll each be pounding 15 nails into wood bases and winding colored wire around the nails to make designs, pictures, words, or whatever they'd like to make. Challenge children to plan out their designs by drawing them on paper.

2. Use pencils to lightly draw a design on each wooden base. Hammer 15 nails in strategic places around each design. (Remind children not to hammer the nails in all the way so that they'll have room to wrap wire around the nails. Hammer the nails about ⅛ to ½ of the way into the wooden bases.)

3. Cut lengths of the colored wires and wrap one end around a nail several times before wrapping around the next nail and so on.

4. When the designs are wrapped, cut 6" lengths of wire and wrap them around a pencil, making loose coils. Then slide beads down the coils, bending the ends of the wires slightly to keep the beads in place.

5. Wrap the beaded, coiled springs around different nail heads to give the designs some real whimsy and eye appeal.

6. Use paints to decorate the wooden bases.

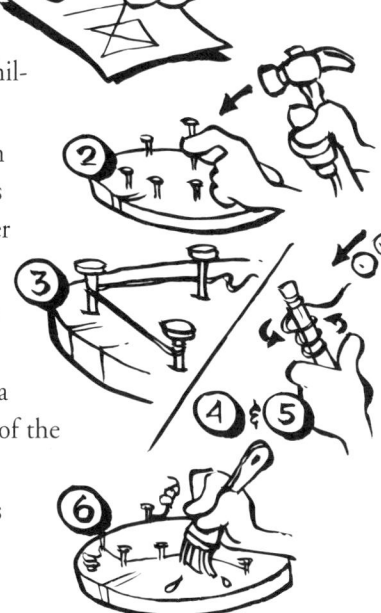

Hammer It Home

Have children take turns showing their designs and their actual projects. Ask them if their plans were achieved and why or why not. Then explain that God has a specific plan for each of them. Whether or not His plans are achieved depends on the choices they make each day. Talk with children about ways they can live faithfully and what God might be able to accomplish as they give their lives over to Him. Challenge them to begin a daily Bible study as a way to learn more about God's plans for their lives.

Bath Salts

15 min.

Grab Your Gear:
- self-locking freezer or storage bags (1 per child)
- large mixing bowls
- mixing spoons
- Epsom salts
- bath salts
- liquid food coloring (in squeeze bottles)
- candy confetti sprinkles
- clear tape
- scissors
- measuring spoons and cups
- curling ribbon
- construction paper
- card patterns from page 51
- photocopier

Note: Before class, photocopy the card patterns from page 51 onto colored construction paper, making one card per child. Cut the cards apart and trim as needed.

Get to Work:

1. Distribute bags, one per child.
2. Work in pairs or trios to mix in bowls the following ingredients for the bath salts: 4 cups Epsom salts, 2 cups bath salts, and 6 drops of food coloring. (These proportions are based on three students per group.)
3. Measure 2 cups of the mixture into each bag. Add one teaspoon of candy confetti sprinkles.
4. Seal the bags securely, and then tape the seals for added security. Distribute the cards and tape one to the front of each bag. Tape lengths of curled ribbon to the bags for a festive touch.

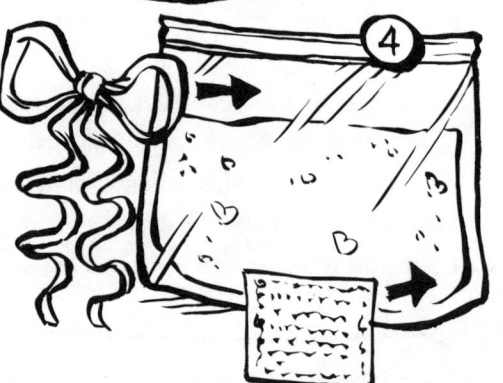

Hammer It Home

Challenge children to present these projects to others as thank-you gifts or simple gestures of encouragement. Talk about different ways that Jesus reached out to love and help those around Him and ways that children can do the same.

Here's a special gift for you
Made with secret "stuff"—
Happy smiles and caring hugs
And love? well, sure enough!
So add these fragrant, soothing salts
To your bath tonight,
Then soak in warmth and lots of love,
And soon you'll feel all right!

Pour 1/2 cup of bath salts under running water.

Here's a special gift for you
Made with secret "stuff"—
Happy smiles and caring hugs
And love? well, sure enough!
So add these fragrant, soothing salts
To your bath tonight,
Then soak in warmth and lots of love,
And soon you'll feel all right!

Pour 1/2 cup of bath salts under running water.

Here's a special gift for you
Made with secret "stuff"—
Happy smiles and caring hugs
And love? well, sure enough!
So add these fragrant, soothing salts
To your bath tonight,
Then soak in warmth and lots of love,
And soon you'll feel all right!

Pour 1/2 cup of bath salts under running water.

Here's a special gift for you
Made with secret "stuff"—
Happy smiles and caring hugs
And love? well, sure enough!
So add these fragrant, soothing salts
To your bath tonight,
Then soak in warmth and lots of love,
And soon you'll feel all right!

Pour 1/2 cup of bath salts under running water.

Here's a special gift for you
Made with secret "stuff"—
Happy smiles and caring hugs
And love? well, sure enough!
So add these fragrant, soothing salts
To your bath tonight,
Then soak in warmth and lots of love,
And soon you'll feel all right!

Pour 1/2 cup of bath salts under running water.

Here's a special gift for you
Made with secret "stuff"—
Happy smiles and caring hugs
And love? well, sure enough!
So add these fragrant, soothing salts
To your bath tonight,
Then soak in warmth and lots of love,
And soon you'll feel all right!

Pour 1/2 cup of bath salts under running water.

Candy Care-Pops

20 min.

Grab Your Gear:
- construction paper (various colors)
- individually wrapped lollipops (flat-sided; 5 per child)
- 4" plastic flowerpots (1 per child)
- modeling or florist's clay
- raffia or ribbon (½" wide)
- curling ribbon
- clear tape
- white craft glue
- bowls of water
- colored tissue paper
- foam brushes
- scissors
- markers
- newspaper
- flower patterns from page 53
- photocopier

Note: Before class, mix one part glue to one part water in mixing bowls or disposable containers. Photocopy the flower patterns from page 53 on colored construction paper, making five flowers per child.

Get to Work:

1. Cover tables with newspaper and give each child a plastic pot. Tear pieces of tissue paper and use foam brushes or fingers to glue the pieces to the pots.
2. When covered, spread another thin layer of glue over the pots. Set aside.
3. Distribute copies of the flower patterns and have children cut out five flowers apiece. Children may trade with each other to allow for color variety.
4. Glue lollipops to the paper flowers. At the tops of the flowers, write: *compassion, kindness, humility, gentleness,* and *patience.* Tie curling ribbon to the sticks and curl the ribbon ends.
5. When the pots are dry (or nearly dry), put clay in the bottoms. Gently stick the ends of the pops into the clay.
6. Tie ½" raffia or ribbon bows around the pots.
7. Cut cards from construction paper and write the following verse on them: *"Clothe yourselves with compassion, kindness, humility, gentleness, and patience." Colossians 3:12.* Tape the cards to the ribbon bows.

Hammer It Home

Talk about each of the words on the Care-Pops and ask children to give examples of times when they've either shown that characteristic or have seen someone else do so. Remind them that Jesus spent His entire life on earth helping and caring for others in many different ways. Challenge them to give their Care-Pops away to others who need a bit of tender loving care today.

Pri–Mid

53

Care-For Friends

20 min.

Grab Your Gear:
- old neckties (wide ties are preferable; 1 per child)
- tacky craft glue or fabric glue
- bags of fiberfill (tissue or newspaper will also work)
- craft foam scraps or buttons
- scissors
- felt or fake fur (in a variety of colors)
- ribbon (½" wide)
- black permanent markers

Get to Work:
1. Let each child choose a necktie. Glue shut the narrow ends of the ties.
2. Gently stuff the neckties with fiberfill, tissue, or newspaper. Make the ties rather plump and stuff them all the way up to both ends.
3. Glue closed the wide ends of the ties, holding the stuffing inside. Set the ties aside to dry.
4. Cut ears from felt, foam, or fur. Encourage children to be creative and invent designs that they like.
5. Cut from foam or felt other facial features including eyes, noses, and mouths, or use buttons.
6. When the ends of the ties are dry, glue on the ears and other features.
7. Cut 5" lengths of ribbon (one per child). Have children write the names of their necktie friends on the ribbons using black permanent markers. Then glue the "collars" around the necks of their ties.

Hammer It Home

Let children introduce their new "pets" and dream up fun and outrageous ways to care for them (feeding them lots of pizza or brushing their teeth with orange juice). Tell children that just as there were no two ties alike, no two people are alike either. Then explain that there are many unique and wonderful ways to show others that they care for them (allow for examples). Let children take their Care-For Friends home as reminders to care for all kinds of people in all kinds of ways, just like Jesus does.

Friends and Family Fences

20 min.

Grab Your Gear:
- paint stir sticks (6 per child)
- newspaper
- acrylic or tempera paints
- paintbrushes
- bowls of water
- tacky craft glue
- felt, yarn, tiny buttons, pom-poms, googly eyes, and other craft scraps
- fine-tipped permanent markers
- scissors
- self-adhesive picture hangers
- hot glue gun (optional; for adult use only)
- thin wire (optional; 15" length per person)
- drill (optional)

Note: If you can't locate enough stir sticks, cut thin plywood into 12" x 2" strips.

Get to Work:

1. Give each child six paint stir sticks. Place four of the sticks on a flat surface and glue a fifth stick across the others, a few inches from the top. Then glue a sixth stick across the "fence," about 1" up from the bottom. (Hot glue guns make this step simple and omit the drying time.)

2. Challenge children to think of several people in their circle of family and friends. Have them paint or draw those people's faces on their sticks, one face per stick.

3. After the faces have dried, use fabric scraps, felt, yarn, and other craft items to make hair, caps, and fun clothing for the characters. Leave the lower portions of the sticks plain.

4. Have children use permanent markers to write on each stick one way they can show love or kindness to the person represented by that particular stick.

5. When the sticks are dry, flip them over and attach self-adhesive picture hangers to the backs. (Or drill holes in both ends of the fences and attach lengths of thin wire from one hole to the other.)

Hammer It Home

Let children take turns "introducing" their special fence people and telling how they plan to show kindness to each person. Explain that they should always be adding new people to their circle of family and friends, and that with each new addition come new opportunities for showing God's love. Challenge children to show the kindnesses they've listed during the coming week.

Bright Bird Feeders

35 min.

Grab Your Gear:
- ¼" plywood
- sandpaper
- hot glue guns (for adult use only)
- wood glue sticks
- tempera paints
- paintbrushes
- bowls of water
- newspaper
- clear plastic wrap
- small paper cups
- birdseed
- rubber bands
- bingo daubers or ink stampers (optional)
- bird feeder patterns from pages 57 and 58
- photocopier
- pencil
- saw

Note: Before class, copy the pattern pieces from pages 57 and 58. Cut from plywood one set of eight patterns for each child. Use a pencil to label each piece according to the letters in the pattern. Invite adult volunteers to help with the hot glue guns.

Get to Work:

1. Cover your table(s) with newspaper. Give each child a set of eight plywood pieces for the bird feeder. Use sandpaper to smooth any rough edges.
2. Glue the roof supports (D) to the centers of the bases (A) crosswise.
3. Assemble and glue the sides of the feeders (B) and (C) around the roof supports (D). Then glue the roof slats (E) to the slanted top edges of the roof supports (D). Let the feeders stand while the glue sets.
4. When the feeders are assembled, paint them as desired. Encourage children to use bright colors and fun designs. Use bingo daubers for polka-dots or try stampers to make creative decorations.
5. While children are painting, fill small paper cups with birdseed. Put plastic wrap over the top of each cup and secure with a rubber band to keep it from spilling. Distribute the cups of seed and tell children to place their bird feeders on decks or porches or nail them to fence posts or windowsills, filling them with seeds, nuts, and berries.

Hammer It Home

Ask children why caring for God's creatures is not only fun to do, but important as well. Explain that when they love and treasure something, they want to care for it. Invite children to talk about ways in which God cares for and provides for them. Then challenge children to place their bird feeders in places where they will be reminded of God's love and of how they can show their love for Him by caring for His creation.

A-base (cut 1)

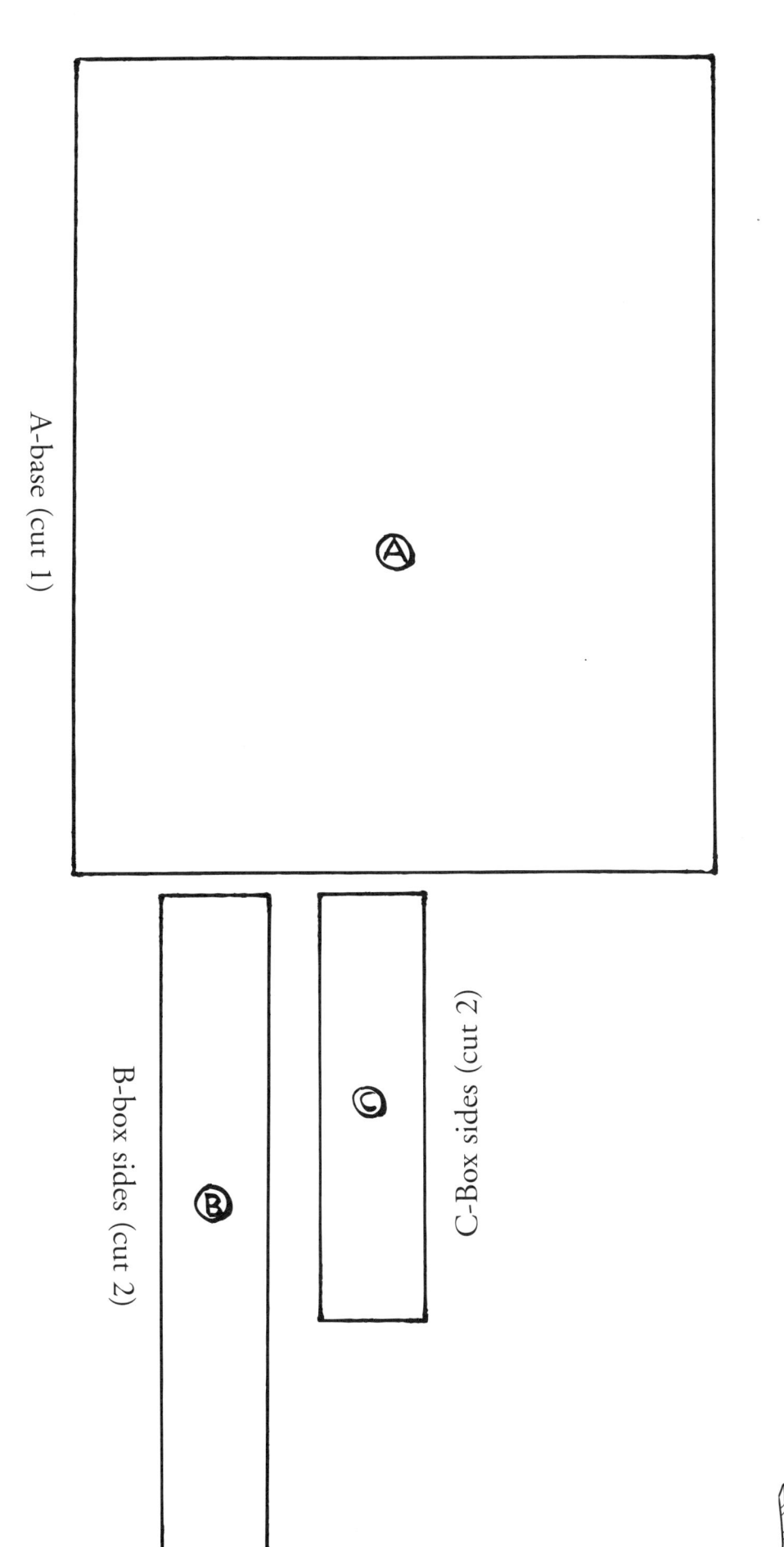

B-box sides (cut 2)

C-Box sides (cut 2)

Pri–Mid

E-roof slat (cut 2)

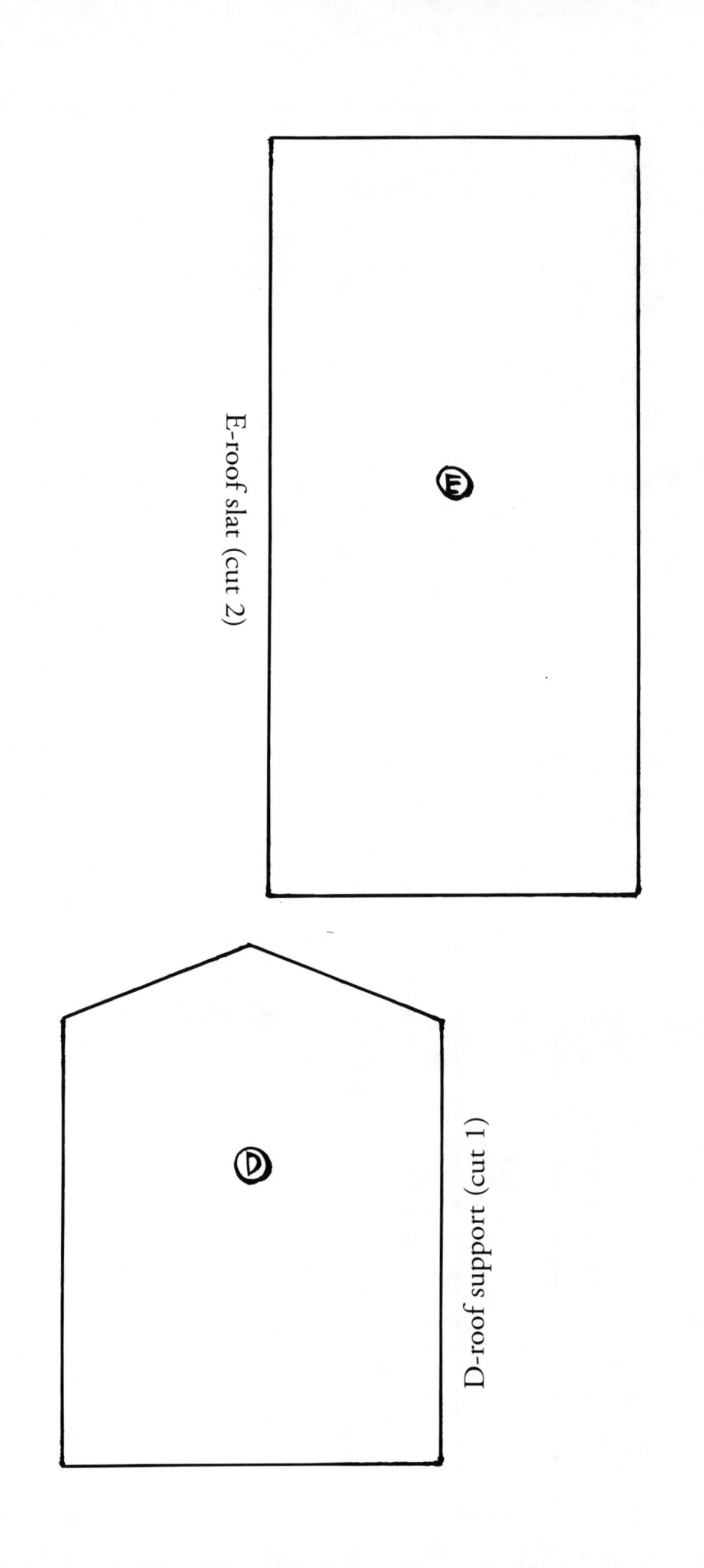

D-roof support (cut 1)

Messages of Forgiveness

25 min.

Grab Your Gear:
- 4" x 12" wooden boards (¾" thick; 1 per child)
- tacky craft glue
- flat sheets of magnetic material (available at most craft stores)
- picture hangers (1 per child)
- 2" decorative flat stones (available at craft stores; 3 per child)
- scissors
- magnetic tape
- red and pink construction paper
- colorful permanent markers
- colorful newspaper comic strips or dried, pressed flowers
- hammers
- ⅝" nails
- hot glue gun

Note: Cut the magnetic sheets into 3" x 11" pieces, one per child. If you can't find these sheets, use rolls of cork and hot-glue the stones to the heads of thumbtacks.

Get to Work:

1. Distribute magnetic (or cork) sheets and the boards. Glue the sheets to the boards. (Older children may wish to nail theirs in place.)
2. If using the magnetic sheets, use hammers and nails to poke holes around the outside edges as borders. (If you're using cork, use permanent markers to decorate its edges.)
3. Flip over the boards and nail or glue picture hangers to the center top edges.
4. Choose fun pictures or faces from the comics, cut them out, and glue them on the stones using a thin layer of tacky craft glue. Each child should make three.
5. While the stones are drying, cut ½" lengths of magnetic tape and attach one piece to the back of each stone.
6. Have each child cut out three 3" red or pink paper hearts. On each heart, write one of the following: *Please forgive me*; *I forgive you*; and *Thanks for forgiving me*! Decorate the hearts using markers.
7. Attach the hearts to the boards using the magnets (or to the corkboard using thumbtacks).

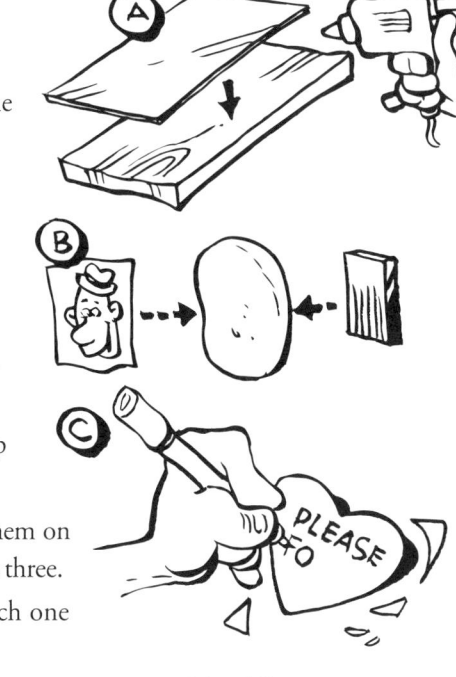

Hammer It Home

Ask children to talk about times they may have asked for forgiveness. Point out that it's often very hard to say "I'm sorry," just as it can also be hard to forgive someone. Remind children that forgiveness is a demonstration of love and that they should ask for forgiveness and give it as well. Have children take their message boards home and use them to post messages when forgiveness is needed.

Stacker-Tac-Toe

⏰ **20 min.**

Grab Your Gear:
- 9" white foam-board squares (1 per child)
- wooden golf tees (9 per child)
- large, flat metal washers (24 per child)
- bright permanent markers
- pencils
- letter-size envelopes
- rulers
- tacky craft glue

Get to Work:

1. Give each child a foam-board square. Use rulers and pencils to draw on each board a grid of three rows with three squares per row.

2. Color the squares as desired. Then write one of the following words at the top or bottom of each square across the first row on their game boards: *ask*, *forgive*, and *repent*. Repeat this order for the middle and bottom rows. (Be sure to write at either the top or bottom of each square, as the tees will be glued in the center!)

3. Flip over the boards and glue envelopes to the backs, with the envelope flaps facing outward. (The envelopes will store the flat playing pieces later.) When the envelopes are in place, flip the boards back over.

4. Distribute wooden golf tees. Turn the tees upside down and glue the heads to the center of each small square on the boards.

5. Give each child 24 flat metal washers. Use markers to color 12 of the washers one color and 12 a second color. (Color both sides of the washers.)

6. The washers are the game pieces and this game is played much like tic-tac-toe. Alternating turns with another player, drop washers over the tees until one color is in a row horizontally, diagonally, or in four corners. For a fun variation, stack one color over another. Store the washers in the envelopes on the backs of the game boards.

Hammer It Home

Let children find partners and play a few rounds of the game as time allows. As they play, talk with them about what the words on their game boards mean. Ask them to give examples of times they've asked for forgiveness, forgiven others, and repented of wrong behavior. Remind them that God is always ready and willing to forgive them and they should offer the same kind of loving forgiveness to others.

Golden Rulers

15 min.

Grab Your Gear:
- small self-adhesive craft foam stars and hearts (2 of each per child)
- 2" jewelry bar pins (1 per child)
- hot glue gun with glue or tacky craft glue
- wide craft sticks (1 per child)
- fine-tipped black permanent markers
- rulers
- gold glitter glue pens
- Bible

Get to Work:

1. Distribute craft sticks. Place rulers beside the craft sticks and use fine-tipped permanent markers to mark off the inch and half-inch lines on the craft sticks. Number the inch marks on the sticks.

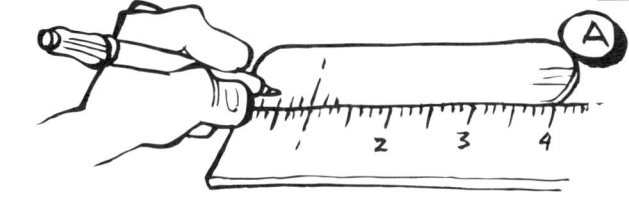

2. Let each child choose two self-adhesive stars and hearts. Stick the stars on the left ends of the craft-stick rulers, positioning them so that one star is on top of the other, slightly off center. (This will give a double star look. Some numbers might be covered, which is fine.)

3. Repeat the same procedure with the hearts, positioning them on the right ends of the craft-stick rulers.

4. Using fine-tipped permanent markers, write the following slogan on the craft sticks: *Forgive others as Jesus forgives us!* On the star shapes, write: *Ephesians 4:32;* on the heart shapes, write: *Colossians 3:13.* If needed, abbreviate the names of the books.

5. Glue the bar pins to the backs of the craft-stick rulers using a hot glue gun or tacky craft glue. Then trim the fronts of the pins with gold glitter glue.

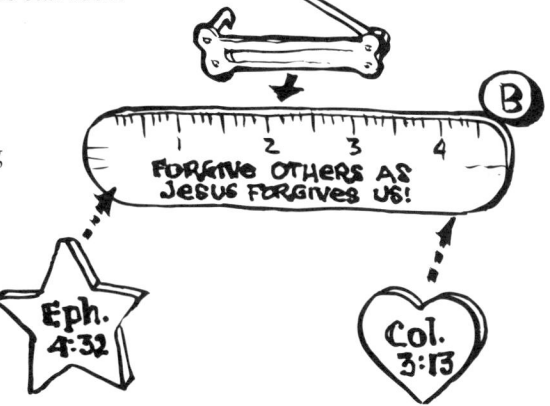

Hammer It Home

As pins dry, invite volunteers to look up and read aloud Ephesians 4:32 and Colossians 3:13. Ask children why it is important to forgive others as Jesus forgives them. Remind them that forgiveness is an act of love, and when they forgive others, they show love to them and to Jesus. Challenge children to wear their pins each day of the coming week to remind themselves and others to forgive as they've been forgiven.

5th/6th graders
- Are beginning their growth spurts and consequently will suffer mood swings.
- Love competition but often lack confidence in their abilities.
- Are strongly motivated by peer pressure and are looking for heroes to imitate.
- Appreciate some attention but are uncomfortable with outwardly emotional displays of affection or attention.

Teens
- Are growing rapidly and becoming more sexually aware.
- Are developing their own self-concepts and need to be accepted for who they are.
- Put up fronts sometimes and can be outwardly cruel to each other.
- Need significant Christian adult examples who are not afraid to confront them if needed.

So . . .
- Provide projects that will sufficiently challenge the students but will be fun too.
- Plan adequately—for the project itself and for those students who finish quickly.
- Provide opportunities for bonding and sharing together during craft time.
- Be an example of Christian love, which may be a real challenge! Don't take literally everything a young teen says. Don't be afraid to confront or talk with your students; they can spot a counterfeit a mile away.

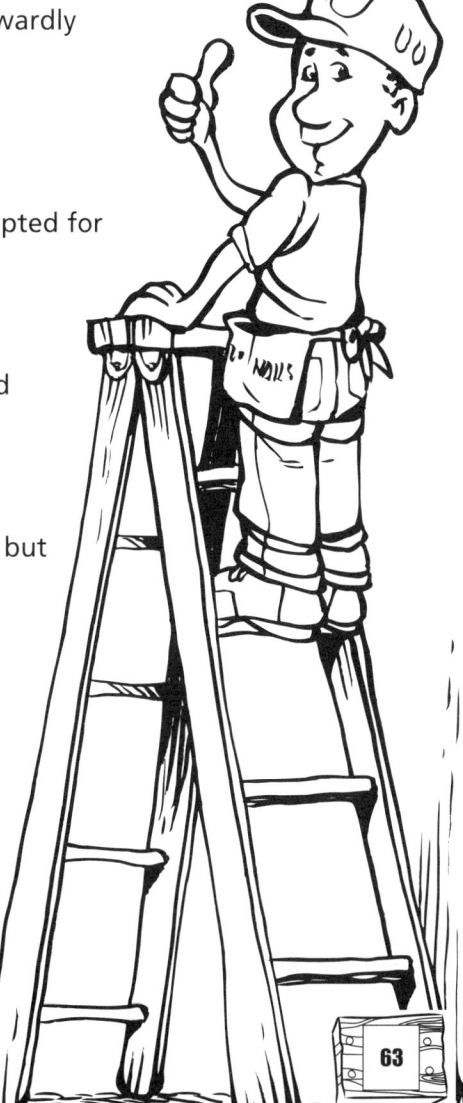

God Rules Tees

20 min.

Grab Your Gear:
- light-colored T-shirts (1 per child)
- small washers (8 per child)
- medium washers (10 per child)
- extra large washers (1 per child)
- rulers (cut in thirds; 1 segment per child)
- small nuts (3 per child)
- medium nuts (13 per child)
- thumbscrews (2 per child)
- small bolts (3 per child)
- large bolts (1 per child)
- large staples (1 per child)
- small angle irons (1 per child)
- spray paint (various colors)
- fabric markers
- sheets of heavy cardboard

Get to Work:
1. Smooth out the shirt and place a sheet of heavy cardboard inside to prevent bleeding of the paints.
2. Use the illustration to place the pieces of hardware on the shirt, spelling out "God Rules." Place a ruler segment between the words as shown.
3. Spray paint over the items onto the shirt. Allow paint to dry.
4. Remove the objects and embellish the shirt with fabric markers as desired.
5. Allow shirt to dry 48 hours before washing inside out.

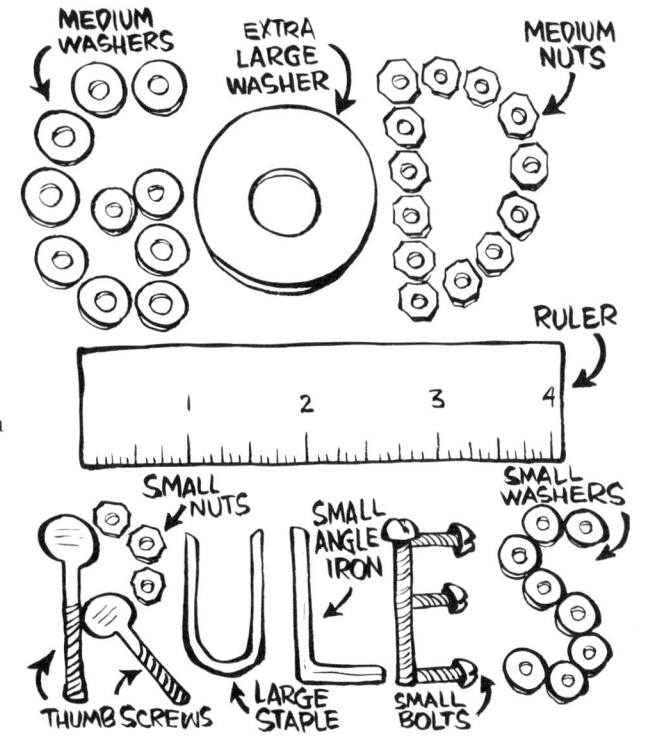

Hammer It Home

As children work, talk about different ways they can build their lives to be more like Jesus and why it is sometimes a struggle. Tell them to wear these shirts as a witness statement to others, as well as a reminder to themselves that no matter what they're going through, God is always in control.

whatcha-ma-call-its

25 min.

Grab Your Gear:
- wooden beads in varying sizes (up to 3"; several beads per child)
- Sculpey® or Fimo® modeling clay (in bright colors)
- oven or large toaster oven
- aluminum foil
- baking sheet
- pencils
- colored wire (not vinyl-coated; 12" per child)
- leather or satin cord

Note: Before class, preheat the oven according to the directions on the packages of clay. Cut 12" lengths of colored wire, one per child.

Get to Work:

1. Cover a large wooden bead with a thin layer of clay. Use a variety of colors and designs.
2. Give each child a 12" length of wire. Have him bend the wire in halves, thirds, or fourths, and thread the end loop up through the clay-covered bead. The loop needs to be about 1" long. Make a clay "collar" around the hole on the bead where the wire loop pokes through.
3. Wrap the wire sticking out of the opposite hole around a pencil to shape it into interesting coils and springs.
4. Knead sculpting clay into small balls. Combine colors and make round, square, or other-shaped beads. Each bead needs to be at least ½" thick. Stick the beads over the ends of the wire on the large bead, making sure the small beads fit tightly. Place the projects on a foil-covered baking sheet and bake according to package directions.
5. Once the clay and wires have cooled, thread 18" lengths of satin or leather cord through the top loop of each wire and tie the ends.

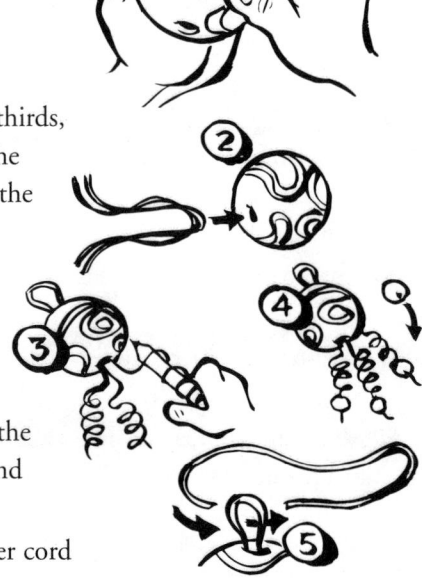

Hammer It Home

Let children compare projects and talk about different ways the colors were used. Talk about how plain the beads would have been if done in only one color. Then point out that, just as the different colors work together to make a pleasing project, Christians become pleasing to God when they build their lives around a variety of qualities (such as humility, obedience, faithfulness, caring, and forgiveness). Children can wear these projects as pendants, attach them to key chains, or suspend them from windows at home as reminders of how God shapes, forms, and fires them as they become more like Jesus.

Humble Houses

45 min.

Grab Your Gear:
- ¼" plywood
- saw
- pencil
- sandpaper
- wood glue
- ⅝" nails or brads (with small heads)
- hammers
- acrylic paints or stain
- paintbrushes
- newspaper
- medium-sized "O" hooks (used for picture hanging; 1 per child)
- scissors
- string
- hay or dried grass
- patterns from pages 68 and 69
- photocopier
- spray wood sealant (optional)
- plastic gems, sequins, glitter glue (optional)

Note: Before class, copy the pattern pieces from pages 68 and 69 and cut from plywood one set of seven pieces for each child. Use a pencil to label each piece according to the letters in the pattern.

Get to Work:

1. Give each child a set of seven pieces: front, back, two sides, two roofs, and a perch plank. Smooth any rough edges or splinters.

2. Spread a thin layer of wood glue along the sides of the birdhouse (B). Then nail each side piece (B) to the front (A) and the back (A) pieces. (If you wish to omit the nails, simply glue the pieces together and blow on them to speed drying time.)

3. Nail the perch plank (C) to the bottom of the front and back pieces (A). Then nail the two roof pieces (D) to the tops of the front and back pieces (A).

4. Distribute "O" hooks and screw one hook into the top of each house. Then thread 10" lengths of string through the hooks and tie the ends to make hanging loops.

5. Spread newspaper on the table and paint or stain the birdhouses as desired. (Optional: Embellish the houses with plastic gems, glitter glue, or other craft scraps. Clear wood sealant will add a protective coating to the projects.)

6. Push hay or dried grass through the holes in the houses.

Hammer It Home

Ask children to describe different kinds of birdhouses they may have seen. Point out that no matter how elaborate a birdhouse might seem, even the most basic ones can be effective. Then explain that God created each person with a special design and when Christians live according to His will, even the most ordinary person can have an extraordinary impact for Christ. Let children take these birdhouses home as a reminder to live humbly and effectively for God.

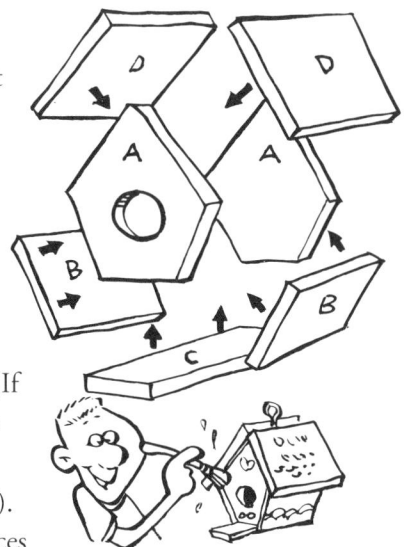

Birdhouse Plans

(Use ¼-inch plywood)

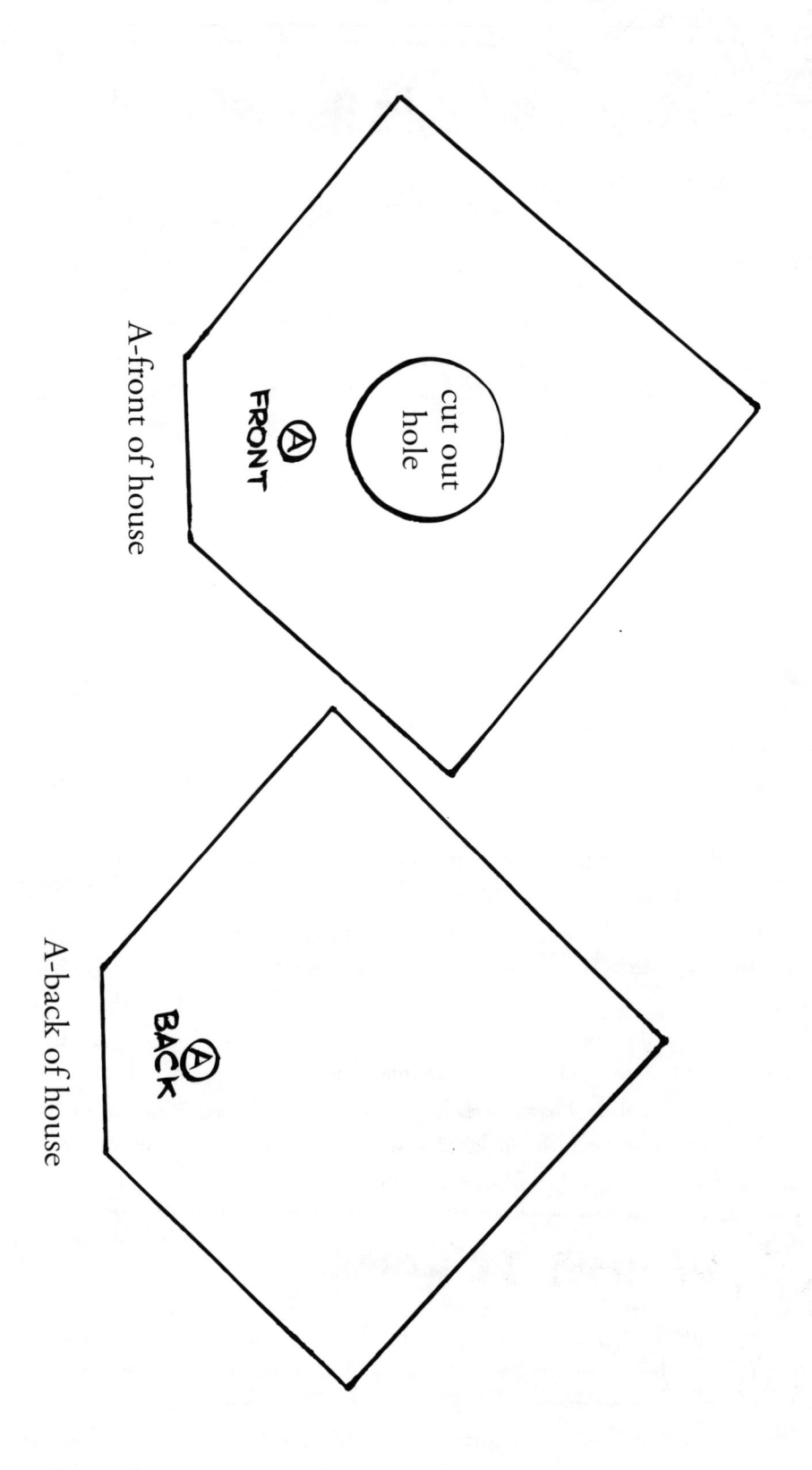

A-front of house

Ⓐ FRONT

cut out hole

A-back of house

Ⓐ BACK

Birdhouse Plans

(Use ¼-inch plywood)

C-Perch Plank (cut 1)

D-roof (cut 2)

B-side of house (cut 2)

5/6–Teen

Nativity Ornaments

20 min.

Grab Your Gear:

- 8½" x 11" clear transparency sheets
- pattern from page 71
- photocopier
- fine-tipped permanent markers (various colors)
- curling ribbon
- scissors
- clear glass or plastic ball ornaments (10¼" circumference; 1 per child)
- several pairs of tweezers
- thin gold cord (6" per child)
- pens

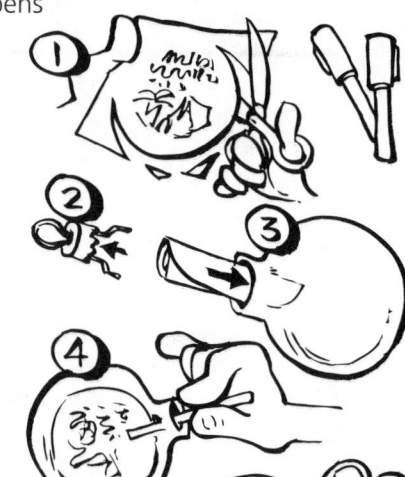

Note: Before class, copy the pattern from page 71 onto clear transparency sheets, reducing or enlarging the artwork as needed to fit your ornaments. Copy two circles per child to allow for mistakes. Cut gold cord into 6" lengths, one per child.

Get to Work:

1. Give each child a circle with a nativity scene. Use fine-tipped permanent markers to color the scenes as desired, and then trim the circles as needed.
2. Distribute the ornaments and carefully remove the metal ends.
3. Tightly wrap the clear nativity circles around pens and carefully insert them into the insides of the ornaments.
4. Use tweezers to position the artwork in place inside the ornaments. The circles should sit upright in the balls and be nearly invisible except for the colored scenes and words. (If a picture doesn't sit in the center of a ball or doesn't quite fit, pull it out, adjust the size of the circle and try again.)
5. After the artwork pieces are in place, recap the ornaments.
6. Thread the cord through the ornament hangers and tie the ends together.
7. Use curling ribbon to tie bows, and then curl the ends with scissors.

Hammer It Home

Briefly review the story of the nativity and talk about the humble manner in which Jesus came to earth. Then discuss reasons why God may have chosen to send His Son in such a manner and what children can learn from His humble beginnings. Remind them that a humble attitude is one way that they can acknowledge the greatness of God and honor Him with their lives. The ornaments can be hung in sunny windows year-round as daily reminders of this important lesson.

"And she brought forth her firstborn Son"

Life's Lessons Plaques

30 min.

Grab Your Gear:
- 8" square wooden bases (½–¾" plywood; 1 per child)
- rolls of soft embossing metal (bronze or aluminum; available at craft stores)
- metal snips or sturdy scissors
- scissors
- lined notebook paper
- pencils
- clear tape
- hammers
- wooden or plastic golf tees (1 per child)
- old rags or soft paper towels
- brown shoe polish (in roller bottles)
- picture hangers
- tacky craft glue
- ½" nails with small heads
- hot glue gun (optional)

Note: Before class, cut the embossing metal into 6" squares (one per child). If you cannot find these rolls of metal, trim the sides from inexpensive foil pie plates and use circular pieces of metal rather than square ones. They'll still work with the square bases.

Get to Work:

1. Give each child a square base and a piece of embossing metal. Stain the plaques by rubbing the wood with shoe polish and then wiping with old rags or paper towels to remove any excess polish.

2. Nail the edges of the metal pieces to the wooden plaques.

3. Distribute lined paper, pencils, and scissors. Trim the papers to match the metal plaques. As a class, brainstorm three rules every family should live by, and state those rules in two-word sentences. Write RULES FOR LIVING across the tops of the papers and list the three rules below. Then tape the papers over the metal pieces and use golf tees to trace the writing. Use firm pressure, tracing the letters one at a time. (Retracing will leave duplicate lines.) Remove the papers.

4. Rub over the words with shoe polish, letting the dye sink into the grooves. Then rub the plaques with rags or towels to remove excess polish. Use glue or nails to add picture hangers to the backs of the plaques.

Hammer It Home

Talk about why rules are important, even when they're hard to follow. Remind children that God provides rules for them, not as a way to control them, but as a way to help them live the full and blessed lives that He intended. While on earth, Jesus modeled these rules through the way He treated others and through His unending love for each of them. Challenge children to hang their plaques where they and their families will see them often and be reminded to follow God's Rules for Living even when it's tough.

wrist Phylacteries

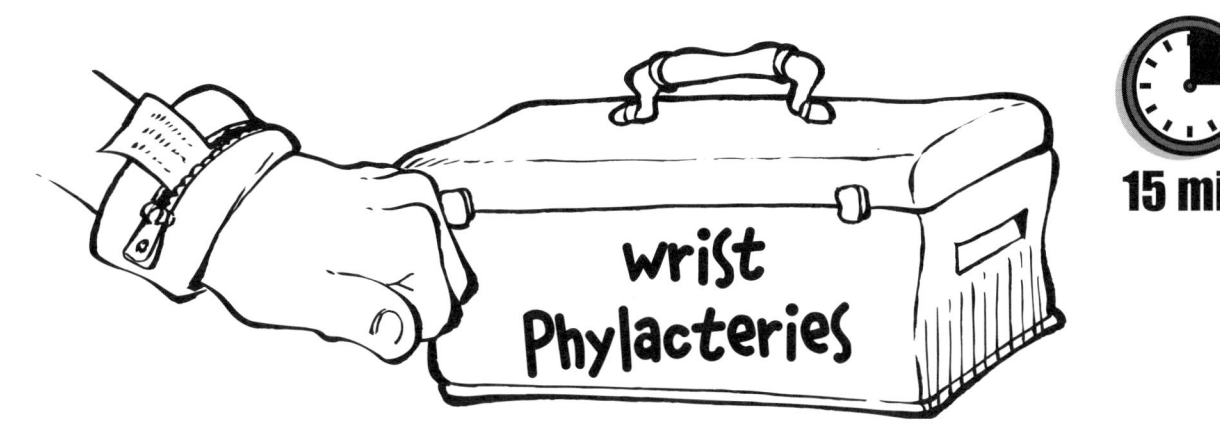

15 min.

Grab Your Gear:
- 8" zippers (in bright colors; 1 per child)
- tacky craft glue or no-stitch fabric glue
- thin craft felt (in a variety of colors)
- scissors
- white copy paper
- pens or fine-tipped markers
- self-adhesive hook-and-loop fasteners (1 set per child)
- fabric paints in small squirt bottles

Get to Work:

1. Distribute the zippers. Cut pieces of craft felt to match the size and shape of the zippers. (This will work best if you keep the zippers closed as you work.)
2. Run a thin bead of glue around the underside edges of the zipper. Carefully line up the zipper over the felt and glue the two pieces together.
3. Use fabric paints to add decorations around the edges of the zippers. Allow to dry.
4. Meanwhile, cut four small slips of paper that will fit inside the zipper once it is opened. (The area between the zipper and the felt backing will make a hidden pocket.) Using pens or fine-tipped markers, write each of the following words or phrases on a slip of paper: *wisdom, stature, favor with God, favor with people*.
5. When the glue and paint on the zippers are completely dry, add self-adhesive hook-and-loop fasteners to the ends of the felt. Children should be able to wrap the strips around their wrists and fasten them.
6. Unzip the secret pockets on the strips, slide the paper slips inside, and then close the zippers.

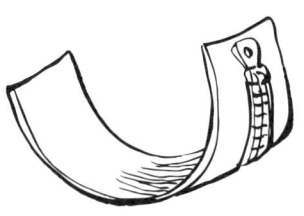

Hammer It Home

Tell children that, in Bible times, some people who studied God's Word actually wore Scripture verses on their bodies in boxes called phylacteries. Phylacteries were made from animal skin, and were attached to leather straps and worn on either the forehead or left hand of a person. The boxes contained pieces of paper with Scripture verses written on them. This was a way of showing that God's Word was so important to these people that they wanted it with them at all times. Talk with children about the importance Jesus placed on God's Word. Then ask a volunteer to read aloud Luke 2:52. Challenge children to use the slips of paper to think of specific ways they can grow as Jesus did.

5/6–Teen

Handy Hold-Its

40 min.

Grab Your Gear:
- ¾" plywood (a 5" x 12" length per child)
- brown liquid shoe polish or furniture polish with dark stain added
- old rags
- ½" nails (wide heads; 5 per child)
- clean, empty baby food jars and lids (4 per child)
- acrylic paints
- small paintbrushes
- small "O" hooks (for picture hanging; 2 per child)
- hammers
- sandpaper
- spray shellac (optional)

Get to Work:

1. Give each child four jars and lids. Paint the outsides of the lids and set aside to dry.
2. Distribute the plywood boards and let children sand the edges. Then rub the boards with polish. Allow the liquid to soak in for several minutes. Use rags to buff the boards and absorb excess polish. Stain the entire surface of the boards and allow them to dry.
3. Place the lids upside down along the length of the boards, spacing them as evenly as possible. (Be sure to leave about ½" at each end.)
4. Nail the lids in place on the boards, hammering one nail through the center of each lid.
5. Flip over the shelves and attach two "O" hooks to the rear corners. (See illustration.) The hooks should simply twist in place.
6. Paint designs on the shelves and jars. Allow paint to dry. (Option: Spray shellac on the shelves to add a bit of gloss and protection.)
7. Have each child place a nail inside one of his jars. Screw the jars into the lids on the shelves. Explain that the shelves can be hung on a wall at home and used to hold jewelry, school supplies, spare change, and other small items.

Hammer It Home

Have children look at the nails in their jars and explain that nails aren't much use when they're locked away. Invite children to compare that to their own faith. Remind them that faith needs to be put into action in order to be useful and effective. Talk about how Jesus demonstrated His faith on a daily basis, and encourage children to think of at least one visible way each of them can put their faith in action today.

Super Serving Spoons

⏱ 15 min.

Grab Your Gear:
- metal or wooden serving spoons (at least 1 per child)
- baking sheets
- aluminum foil
- bowls of soapy water
- old rags
- Sculpey® or Fimo® sculpting clay (in various colors)
- an oven or large toaster oven
- silver polish (optional)

Note: You may also want to have other serving pieces available, such as meat forks, pie servers, or pickle forks.

Get to Work:

1. Preheat the oven according to package directions for the clay.
2. Give each child a spoon. Clean the pieces with soapy water or silver cleaner and dry thoroughly.
3. Cover the handles of the spoons with sculpting clay. Make interesting patterns and designs such as stripes, dots, stars, flowers, or swirls. Be sure to keep the clay tight against the handles and cover them from tip to neck.
4. If you have additional serving pieces available, decorate them in the same manner.
5. Cover the baking sheets with aluminum foil and gently place the serving pieces on the foil. Bake the utensils according to package directions on the clay. Allow pieces to cool before removing them from the sheets. Remind children that these items are not to go in a dishwasher, but must be gently washed by hand without soaking in water.

Hammer It Home

Briefly talk with children about special mealtime traditions in their homes. Explain that meals are often a place of fellowship and sharing among family members. Remind them that meals are not only fun and enjoyable but necessary to their bodies. Then ask children to compare physical feeding to spiritual feeding. Help them understand that, just as their bodies need food to survive, their spirits and minds need the "food" of God's Word. Challenge children to begin a daily Bible study as a way to satisfy their spiritual hunger.

5/6–Teen

Faithful Bookends

35 min.

Grab Your Gear:
- round cardboard containers with lids (oatmeal, corn puffs, or bread crumb canisters work well; 2 identical containers per child)
- nonstick cooking spray
- quick-setting plaster of paris
- masking tape or duct tape
- old bucket
- water
- sponges
- fine-grained sandpaper
- craft felt
- tacky craft glue
- permanent markers
- acrylic paints
- paintbrushes

Note: This project takes only a few minutes to prepare and pour, but plan on several hours or even overnight to allow the plaster to dry completely. If you want smaller bookends, use smaller boxes or containers. Don't use metal or plastic, though, as you'll need to peel away the containers to remove the plaster shapes.

Get to Work:
1. Give each child two identical containers. Remove the lids and inspect the containers carefully to be sure the insides are clean.
2. Spray the insides of the containers with nonstick cooking spray.
3. Mix a large batch of quick-setting plaster of paris according to package directions. (Use an old bucket that can be thrown away when you're finished.)
4. Pour the plaster into the containers, up to about ¾ full.
5. Place the lids securely on the containers and use masking tape or duct tape to seal the edges. Lay the containers on their sides in an out-of-the-way place where they won't be disturbed or roll around. Let plaster dry for several hours or overnight.
6. When the plaster is completely dry, peel or cut away the containers from the bookends.
7. Gently sand any rough areas of the plaster with fine-grained sandpaper. Afterward, brush away any plaster dust or gently rub the bookends with damp sponges.
8. Use permanent markers to write the following words on the bookends: *Faith*, *Hope*, and *Trust*. Then use paints to add designs and patterns to the bookends.
9. Glue craft felt to the bottoms of the bookends to keep them from scratching tables and shelves.

Faithful Bookends

Hammer It Home

Review the words children have written on their bookends. Talk with them about what it means to give themselves over to God completely and to fully trust Him with every aspect of their lives. Remind children that Jesus did just that when He was on earth, and God gave Him strength and courage to endure many hardships. Jesus drew strength from Scripture—which is still available to people today. Encourage children to use these bookends to hold their Bibles, journals, devotionals, and other Bible-study tools as they build stronger, more faith-filled lives.

Caring Cassettes

25 min.

Grab Your Gear:
- clear plastic cassette cases (unscratched; 1 per child)
- magazines or old greeting cards
- tacky craft glue
- scissors
- hot glue gun
- construction paper or card stock (various colors)
- white poster board
- paint pens or permanent markers
- glitter glue
- patterns of verse cards from page 79
- photocopier
- plastic gems, sequins, and decorative braid (optional)

Note: Before class, copy the verse cards from page 79 onto construction paper or card stock (one set of cards per child).

Get to Work:

1. Distribute empty cassette cases. Gently open and fold back the tops of the cases.
2. Look through magazines or old greeting cards to find pictures that would look nice when glued to the backs of the lids. Find pictures that can be trimmed to stand above the top edges of the cases.
3. Glue the pictures to poster board and cut them out. (Remind children to cut so the pictures have straight bottoms and stick up above the case tops!) Attach with glue to the trays on the fronts of the cassette cases.
4. Decorate the backs of the cassette cases using paint pens or markers and glitter glue. Add plastic gems, sequins, and decorative braid as desired. Set the cases aside to dry.
5. Distribute the verse cards and cut them out. Allow children to swap cards so that everyone has a variety of colors, but a complete set of cards.
6. When the cases are dry, stack the verse cards and place them in the trays on the fronts of the cases. (The cut-out pictures should stand above the cards.) Outline the front tray in glitter glue if desired. Allow to dry completely.

Hammer It Home

Invite children to give examples of times when they've been caring or compassionate to someone else, as well as times when others have been caring toward them. Talk briefly about different ways that Jesus showed compassion toward others while on earth. Remind children that caring and compassion are outward demonstrations of their love, not only for others but for God as well. If time allows, review the verse cards together. Children may keep this project as a personal reminder to care for others or give it away as a special way of showing love to someone else.

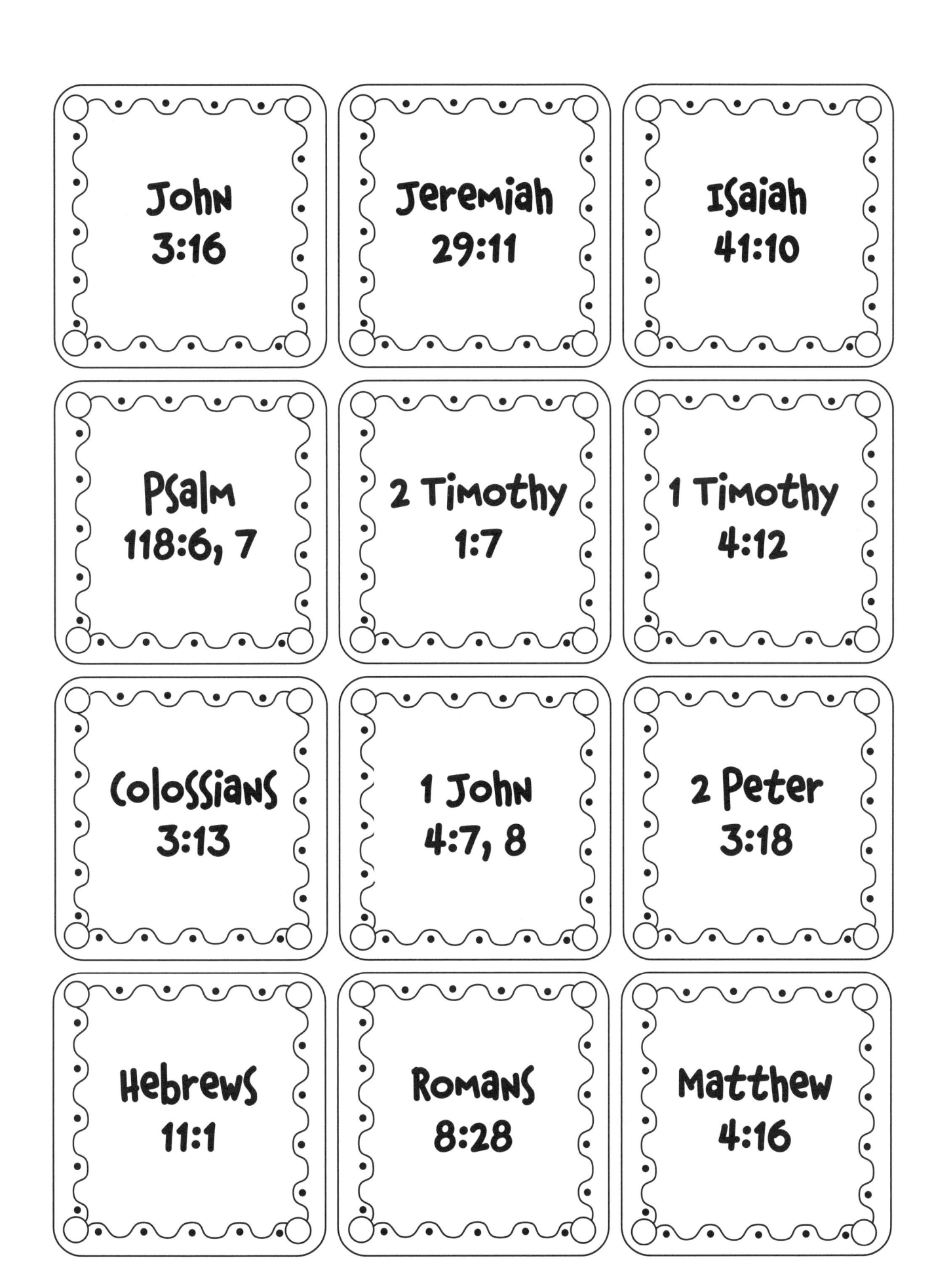

John 3:16	Jeremiah 29:11	Isaiah 41:10
Psalm 118:6, 7	2 Timothy 1:7	1 Timothy 4:12
Colossians 3:13	1 John 4:7, 8	2 Peter 3:18
Hebrews 11:1	Romans 8:28	Matthew 4:16

Funky Photo Frames

20 min.

Grab Your Gear:
- small, square tissue boxes (decorated in wild designs; 1 per child)
- poster board
- pencils
- glitter glue
- 4mm round beads
- thin beading wire
- hot glue gun
- self-adhesive magnetic tape (3" per child)
- scissors
- gold braid or cord
- clear tape
- instant camera and film

Note: Either remove the tissues from the boxes and use them in another box or save up "empties" prior to class. Cut one 18" length of beading wire and one 3" length of magnetic tape for each child.

Get to Work:

1. Give each person a tissue box. Carefully cut the tops off the boxes, removing any cellophane or clear plastic that may be lining the openings. Discard box bottoms.

2. Take group photos of the class, one picture for each child.

3. While the photos are developing, place the box tops on poster board and lightly trace around them with pencils. (These will be the backs of the frames.) Cut out the poster board backs about ¼" larger than the traced lines. (These extra edges will hold the decorative braid or cord.)

4. Distribute the photos and have children tape them behind the holes in the tissue box tops, so that the pictures are centered inside. Then glue the poster board backs to the box tops. (If children wish to change pictures at some point, tell them not to glue the bottom edge.)

5. Glue decorative braid or cord to the slightly larger edges of the poster board backs. Embellish the frames with glitter glue if desired.

6. String beads on 18" lengths of thin beading wire, bending the ends to keep the beads in place. Carefully hot glue the beaded wires to the fronts of the frames or wind them loosely around the edges.

7. Add 3" lengths of self-adhesive magnetic tape to the backs of the frames.

Hammer It Home

Talk with children about the gift of friendship and the impact a friend can have on someone's life. Ask them to name examples of times when the kindness of a friend or family member really encouraged or comforted them. Talk briefly about the ways Jesus reached out to others in kindness and love, and then challenge children to think of people to whom they could show compassion today.

10 min.

Cross Medallions

Grab Your Gear:
- 3" plastic lids (1 per child)
- white craft glue
- small key chains or rings
- thin leather or satin cord
- scissors
- petroleum jelly
- 4mm beads (variety of colors)
- 4mm wooden beads
- thin knitting or darning needle
- blow-dryers (optional, but recommended)

Get to Work:

1. Give each child a plastic lid. Coat the insides of the lids with petroleum jelly.
2. Squeeze a layer of white craft glue into each lid, completely covering the bottom to a depth of about ⅛".
3. Place colored beads in the glue, rimming the outside edges of the lids.
4. Place two rows of wooden beads going down and across the lids, forming crosses in the glue. (Make sure that all the beads in the cross touch each other and that the top, bottom, and sides of the cross touch the outer ring of beads.)
5. Use blow-dryers to speed drying until the glue is clear. (Otherwise, the glue will take about two days to dry.)
6. When the glue is completely clear and hard to the touch, simply pop the medallions out of the lids.
7. Poke a hole at the top of each medallion by inserting a needle through the glue.
8. If children want to make key chains or rings, let them thread those items through the hole in the medallion. For neckwear, have children thread 18" lengths of thin leather or satin cord through the holes and tie the ends.

Hammer It Home

Briefly talk with children about how the glue is holding the beads together, even though it's hard to see. Explain that, because of the forgiveness Christ has offered them, they have the hope of eternity in Heaven—a wonderful promise that is invisible now, but one they can depend on. Encourage children to use these medallions as reminders of the love and forgiveness Christ provides, and as inspiration to offer that same kind of love and forgiveness to others.

Four Nails of Forgiveness

25 min.

Grab Your Gear:
- 4" nails with large heads (4 per child)
- brightly colored yarn
- plastic needlepoint canvas (medium-size squares)
- darning needles with large eyes (1 per child)
- scissors
- fishing line
- cross pattern from page 83
- stiff paper
- photocopier

Note: Before class, copy the cross pattern from page 83 on stiff paper (one copy per child). Enlarge or reduce the size of the pattern to fit on your needlepoint squares, if needed. Rub the sharp points of the nails on a sidewalk to dull them slightly. Cut 6" lengths of fishing line (four per child) and 8" lengths of yarn (one per child).

Get to Work:

1. Give each child a cross pattern, a sheet of needlepoint canvas, and a pair of scissors. Trim out the patterns, lay them on the needlepoint canvas, and use the patterns as guides to cut crosses from the plastic canvas. (Tell children to trim closely beside the squares to avoid little snags that may poke out.)

2. Use darning needles to weave yarn in and out through the squares, filling the cross completely. (Run the ends of the yarn through the stitches at the back of the canvas.)

3. Give each child four lengths of fishing line. Tie fishing line to the head of each nail using a fisherman's knot. (Wrap the line two times around the head of a nail, and then run the end of the fishing line down through the two "wraps" and pull snugly.)

4. Tie the loose ends of the fishing line pieces to the cross as illustrated. Then tie loops of yarn to the tops of the crosses for hanging. (You may need to use the darning needles to do so.)

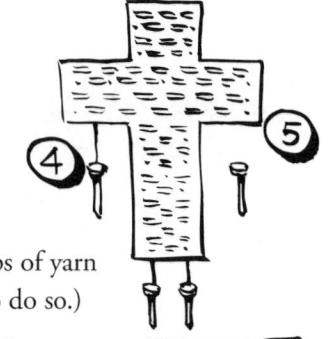

Hammer It Home

Explain that each of the four nails on the cross represents a different aspect of forgiveness: Point to a nail on the crossbeam and tell children it stands for asking forgiveness for themselves; point to the nail on the other end and tell them it stands for forgiving their family members; a third nail stands for forgiving friends and neighbors; the fourth stands for forgiving strangers or enemies. Tell children to hang their crosses where they'll be reminded of the "four nails of forgiveness" each day!

83

REPRODUCIBLES

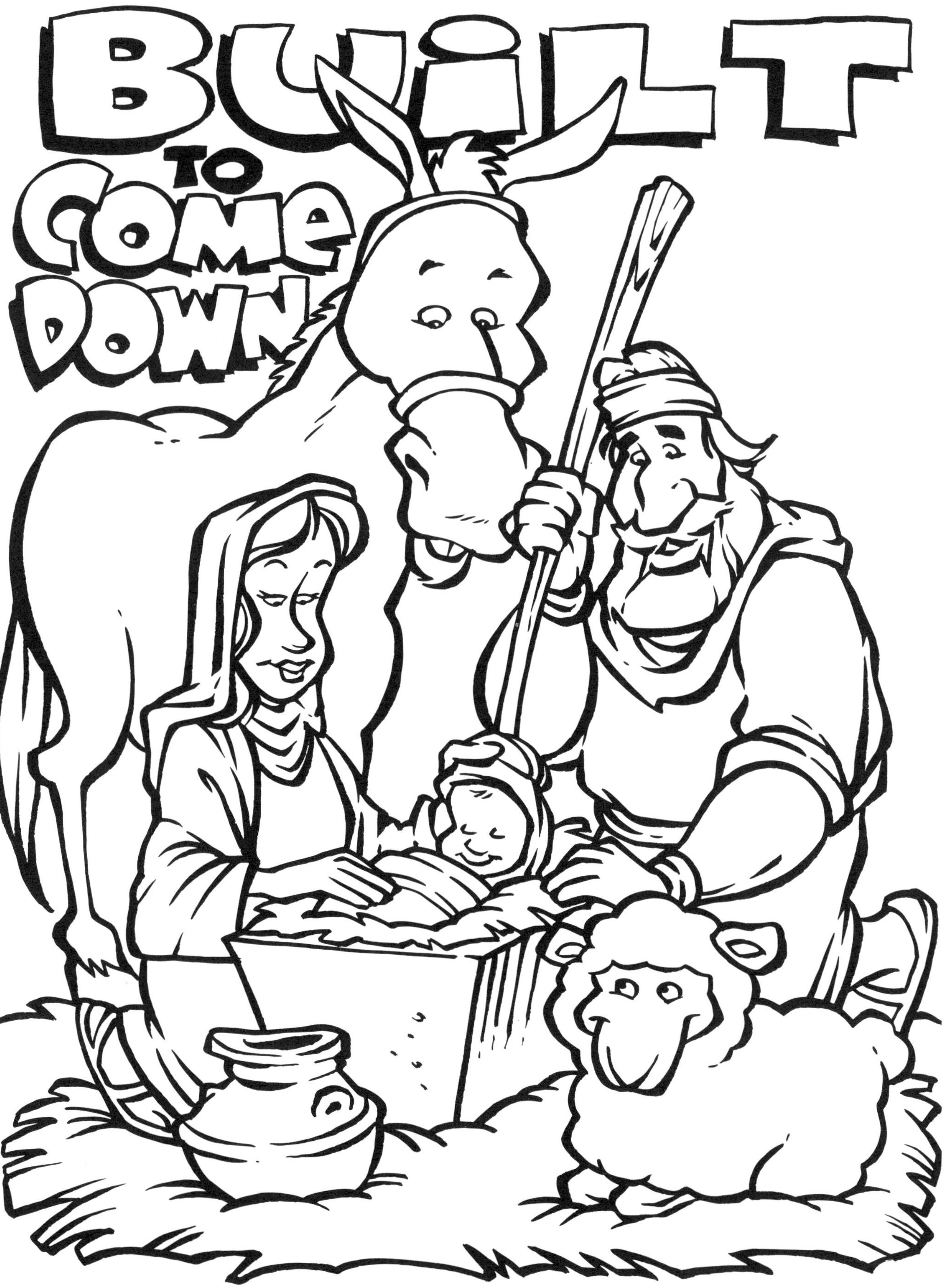
BUILT
TO
COME
DOWN

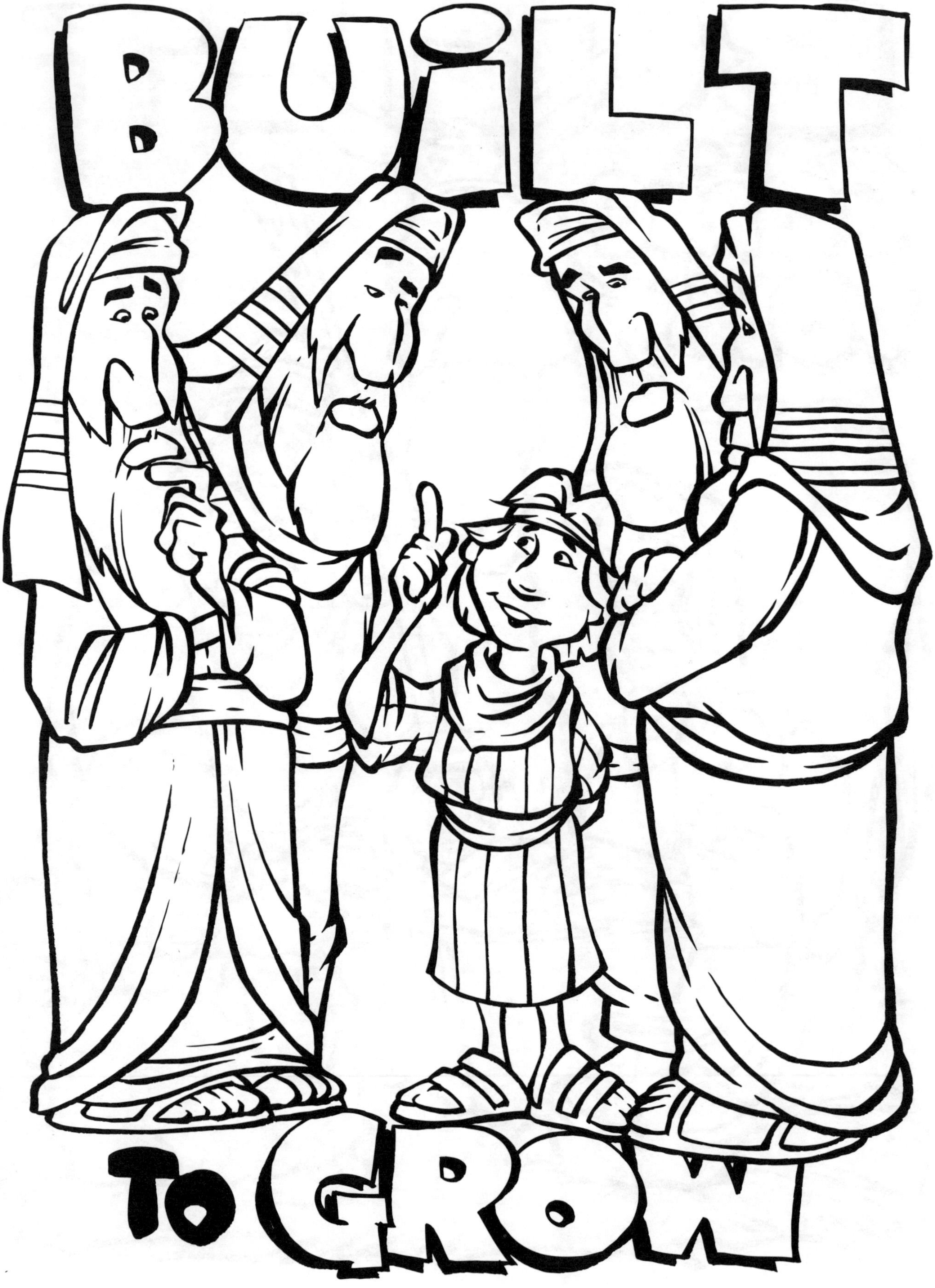
BUILT
TO GROW

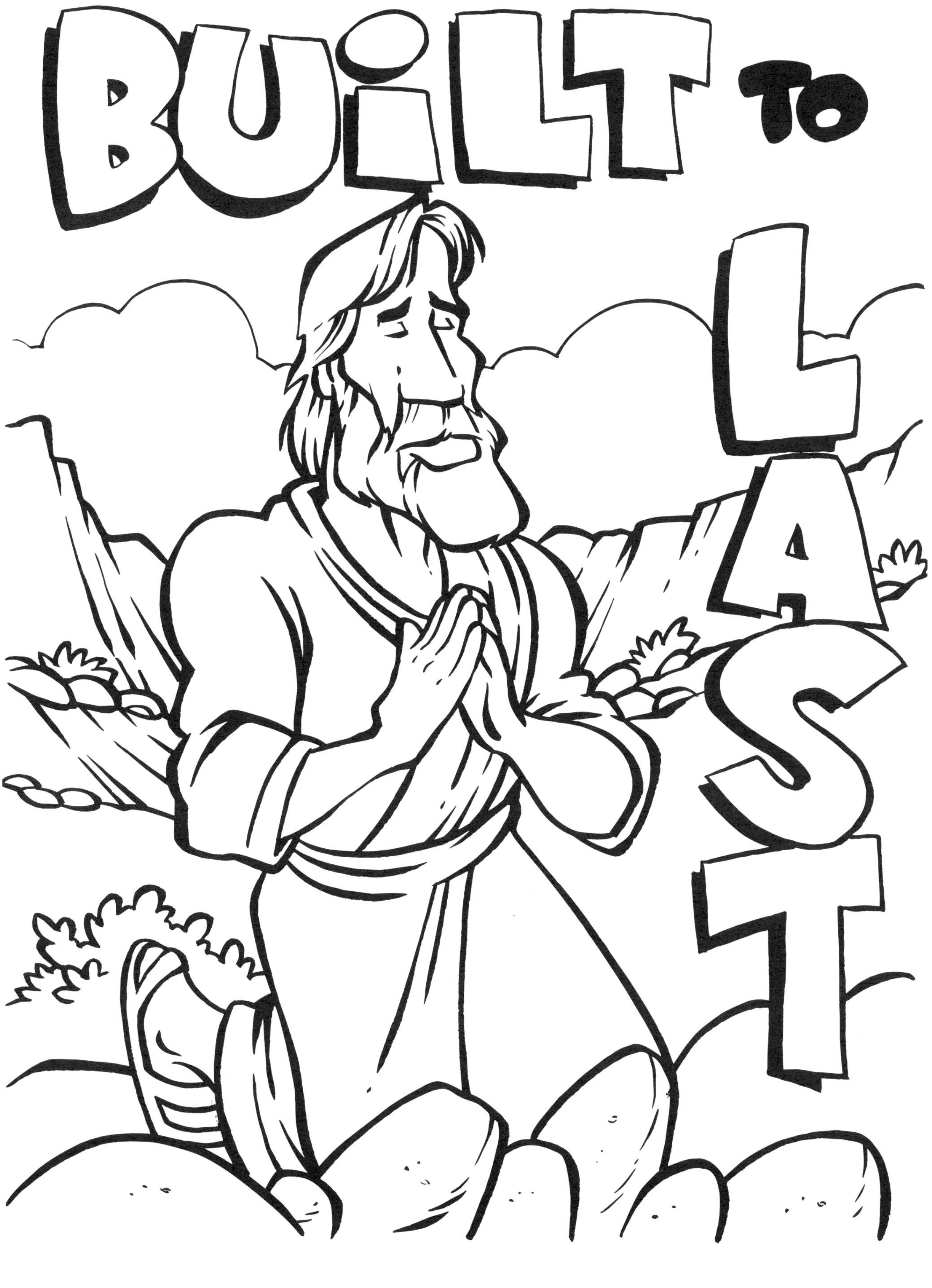
BUILT TO
LAST

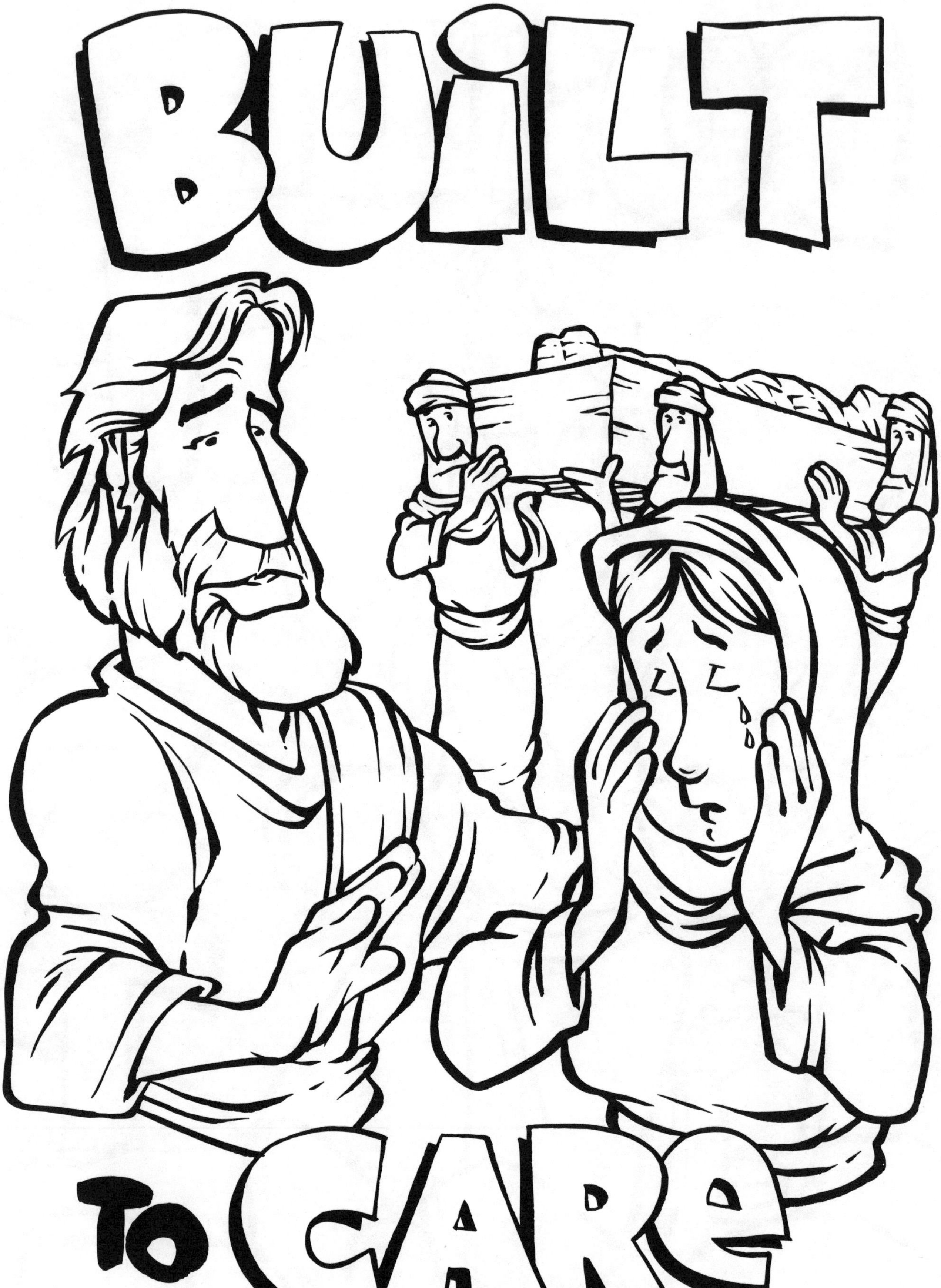
BUILT
TO CARE

BUILT TO RESTORE

BE OBEDIENT JUST LIKE JESUS

BE FAITHFUL

JUST LIKE JESUS

BE CARING
JUST LIKE JESUS

Be Forgiving Just Like Jesus

97

CAULK

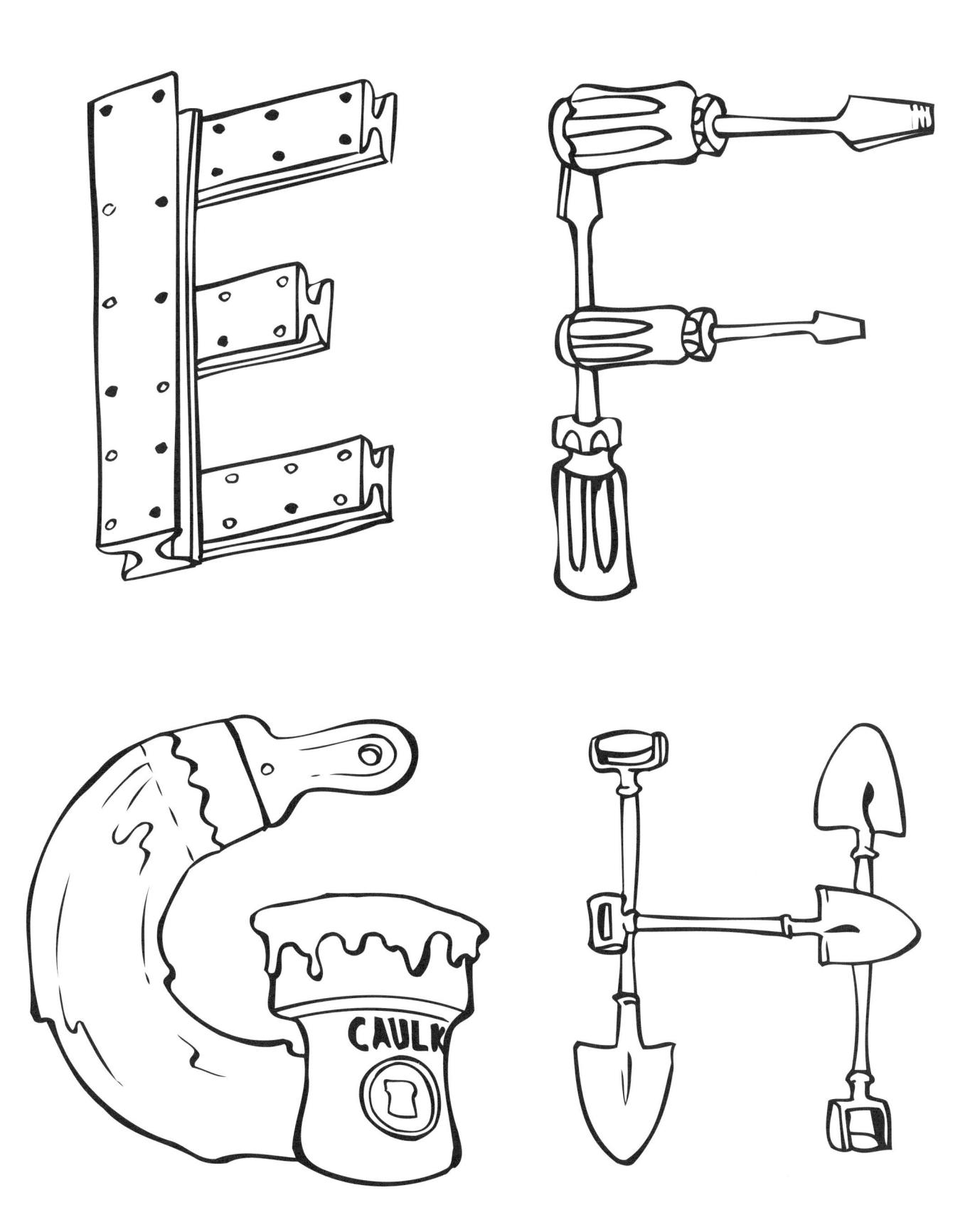

99

101

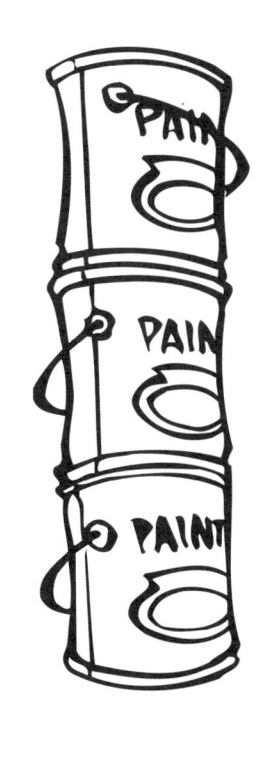

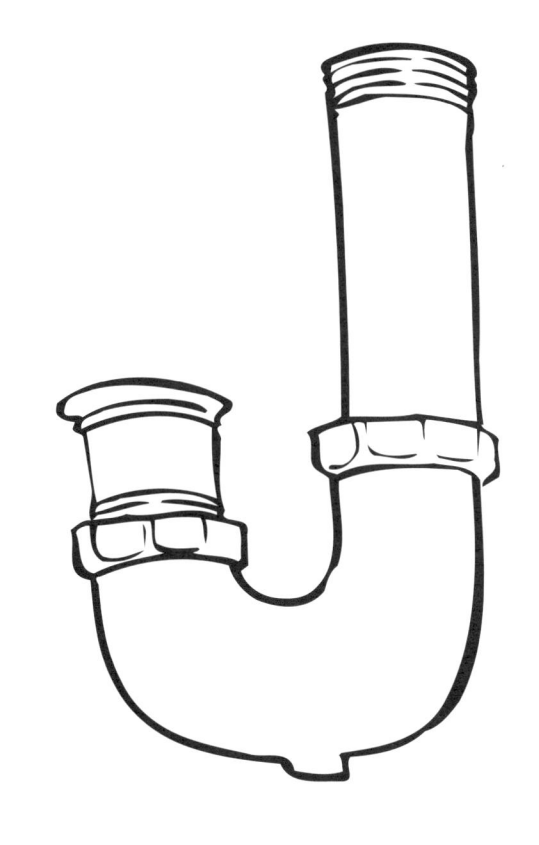

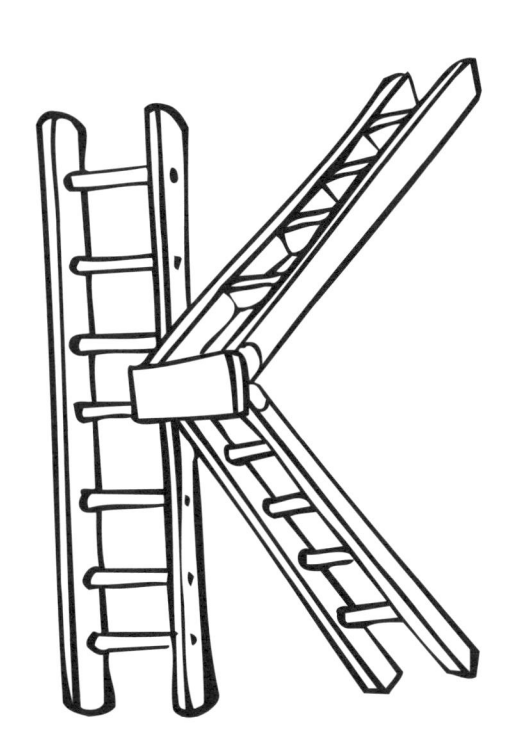

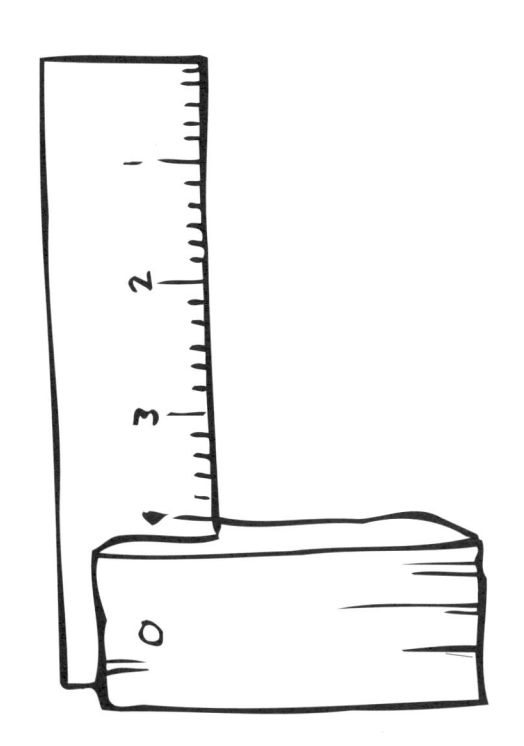

M N
O P

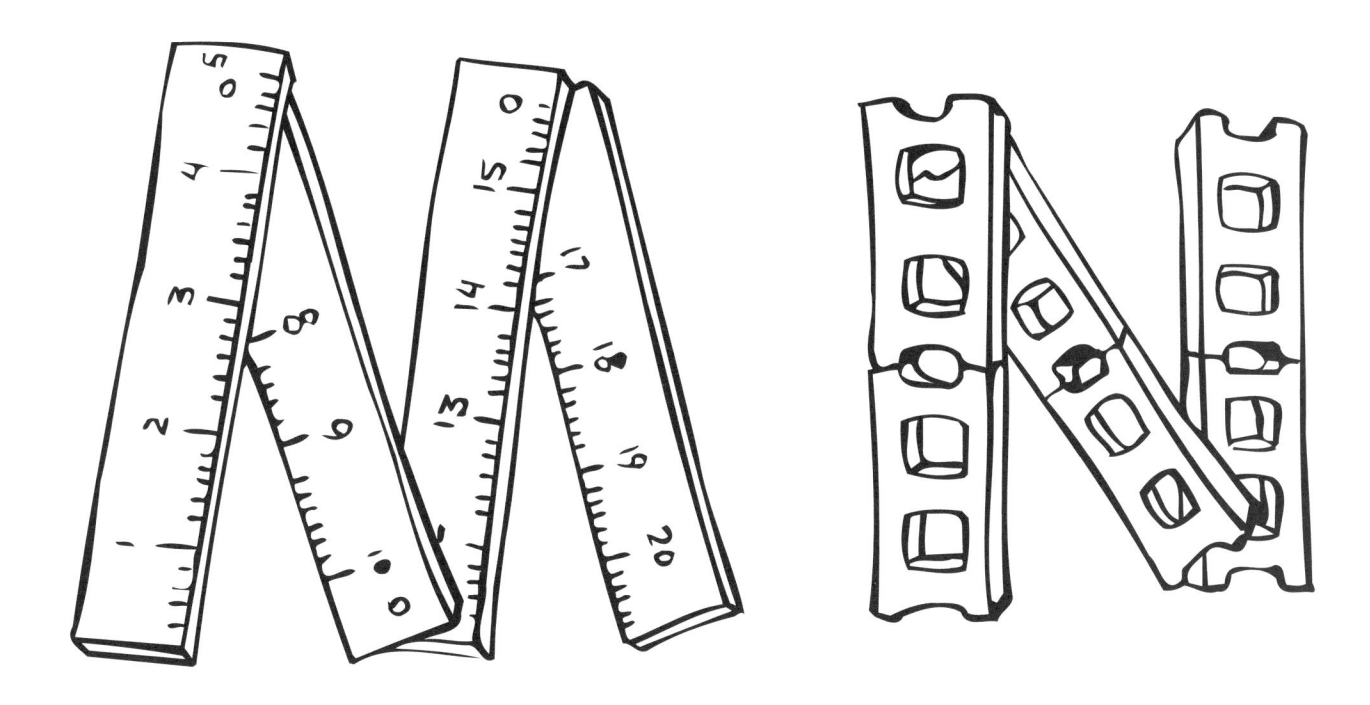

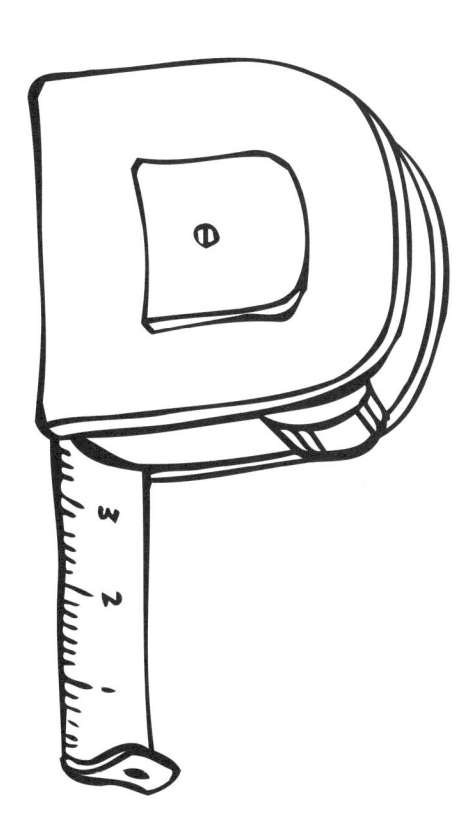

105

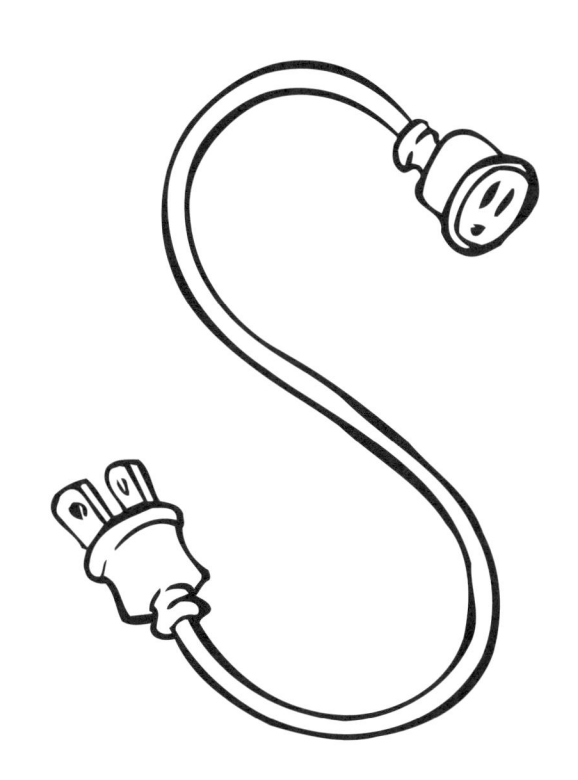

107

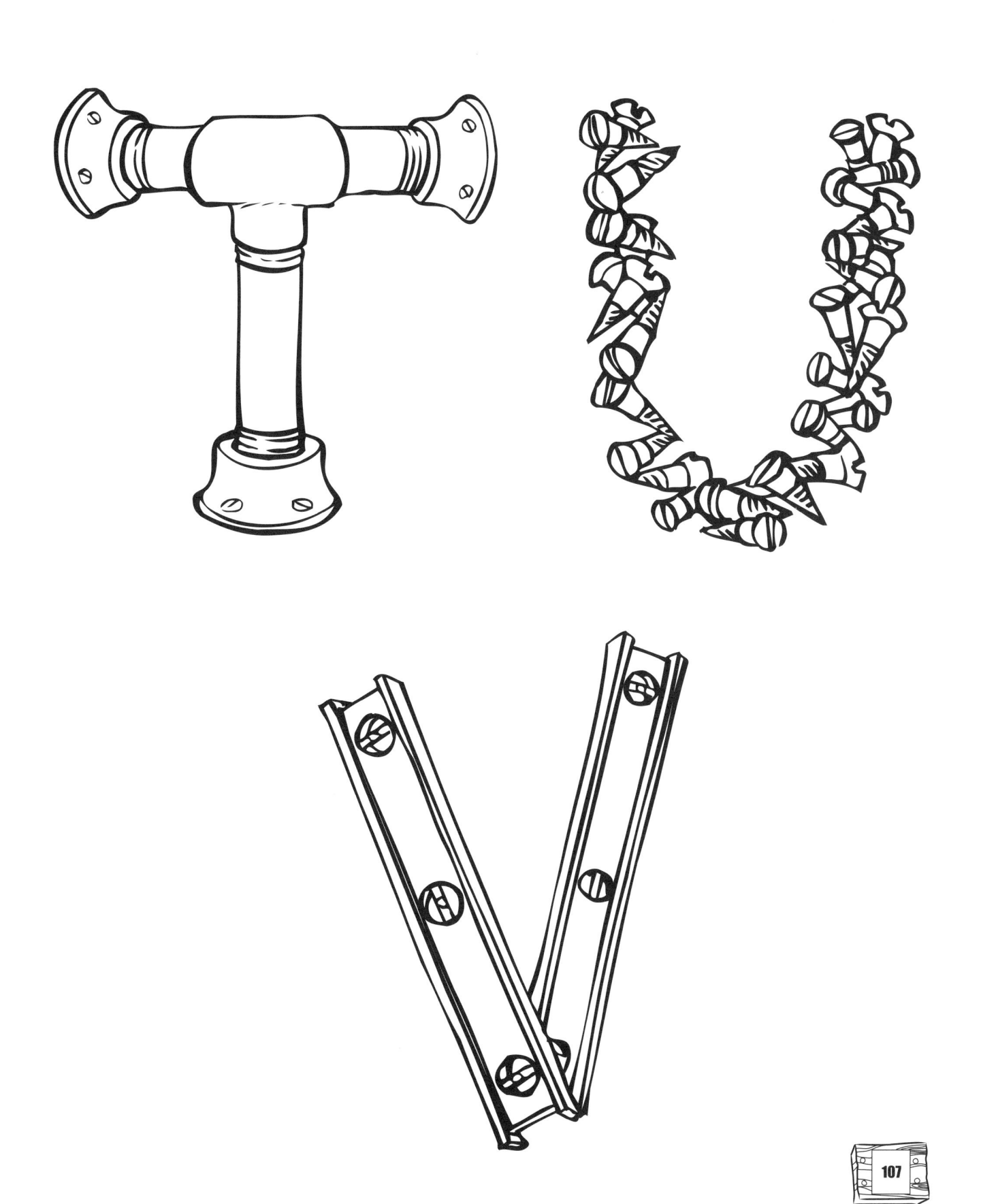

109

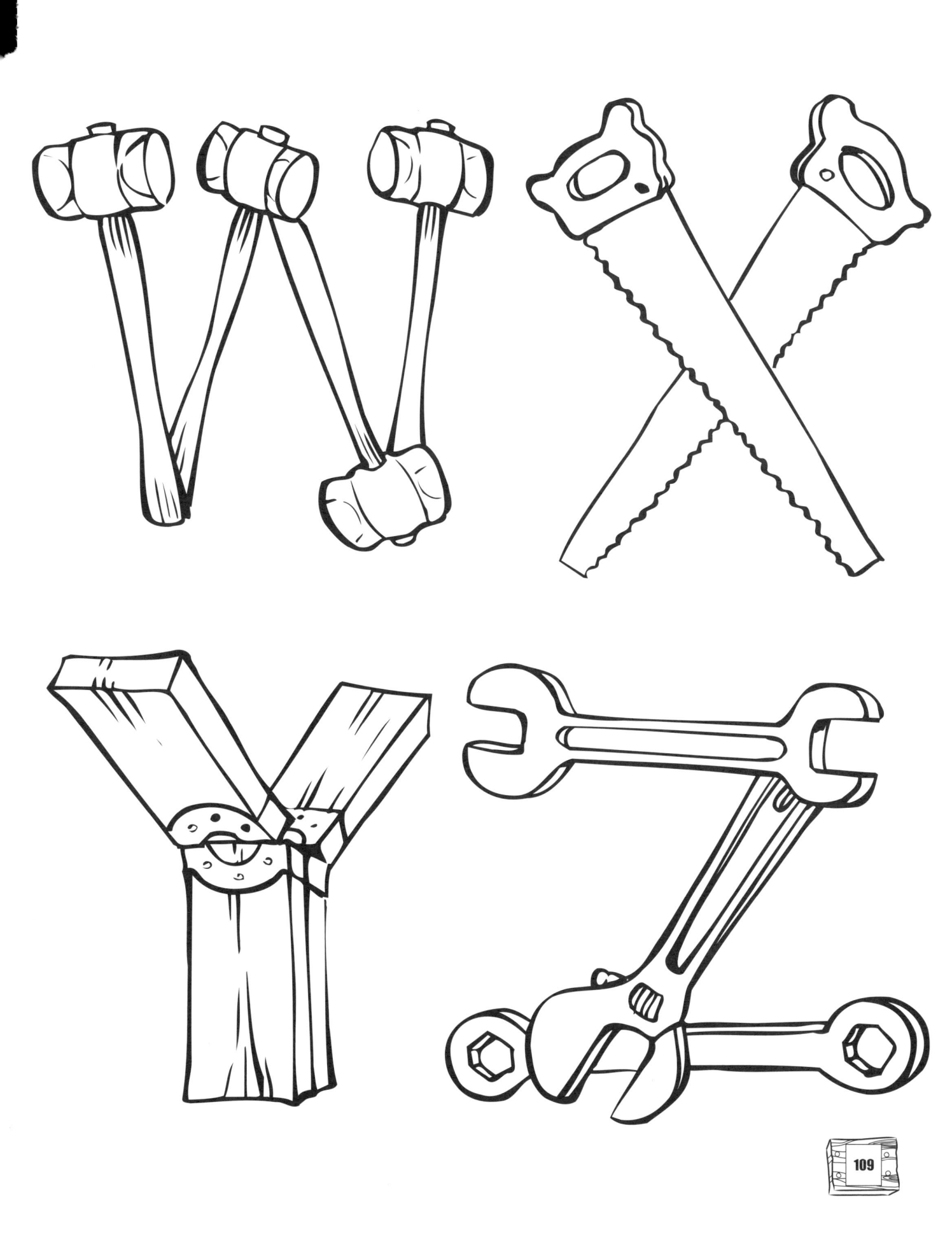

Award of Excellence

Presented to

Name: _____

Date: _____

From: _____

Signed: _____

"Building Character Like Jesus!"

Outstanding Achievement Award

AWARD — Outstanding Achievement

Presented to

Name _____

From _____

Date _____

Signed _____

Building Character Like Jesus!